John Caple, Ph.D., is a career counselor and professor with degrees in economics and business administration from Stanford and Harvard. He leads workshops for clients ranging from IBM to Esalen Institute.

A GUIDEBOOK TO SUCCESS
IN THE PASSAGES AND CHALLENGES
OF YOUR WORK LIFE

CAREER-CYCLES

JOHN CAPLE

A SPECTRUM BOOK

Prentice-Hall, Inc., Englewood Cliffs, New Jersey 07632

Library of Congress Cataloging in Publication Data

Caple, John.
   Careercycles : a guidebook to success in the passages
and challenges of your work life.

   "A Spectrum Book."
   Bibliography: p.
   Includes index.
   1. Vocational guidance.   2. Career changes.
3. Success.   4. Job satisfaction.   I. Title.
HF5381.C263 1983   650.1   83-13658
ISBN 0-13-114587-8
ISBN 0-13-114579-7 (pbk.)

1 2 3 4 5 6 7 8 9 10

ISBN 0-13-114587-8
ISBN 0-13-114579-7 {PBK.}

Editorial/production supervision by William P. O'Hearn
Cover design by Ben Santora
Manufacturing buyer: Doreen Cavallo

This book is available at a special discount when ordered in
bulk quantities. Contact Prentice-Hall, Inc., General
Publishing Division, Special Sales, Englewood Cliffs, N.J. 07632.

Prentice-Hall International, Inc., *London*
Prentice-Hall of Australia Pty. Limited, *Sydney*
Prentice-Hall Canada Inc., *Toronto*
Prentice-Hall of India Private Limited, *New Delhi*
Prentice-Hall of Japan, Inc., *Tokyo*
Prentice-Hall of Southeast Asia Pte. Ltd., *Singapore*
Whitehall Books Limited, *Wellington, New Zealand*
Editora Prentice-Hall do Brasil Ltda., *Rio de Janeiro*

To all those who have taught me about work:
family, students, teachers, colleagues, clients,
and other friends

CONTENTS

FOREWORD

Careercycles is a particularly important book right now. It moves beyond the superficial, how-to-do-it, stay ahead of the pack, success and survival handbooks that have flooded the media marketplace in the past few years. This work traces real passages that all of us experience in our personal development, and it illuminates important relationships between natural cycles and career cycles. It adds new depth to career topography.

Economic and social change, of the level now in world experience, is both exhilarating and terrifying. Dealing with career/life change in response to external factors is one of the most challenging occupations we all face. Traditionally, most of us settle into career directions that are (or appear) predictable, secure, and somewhat mechanical in day-to-day application: the ladder to the top, the organizational survival maze, a career path of hallways and doors followed by longer hallways and doors sometimes leading to plateaus, burnout, and psychic retirement.

Although there is nothing wrong with a planned, secure career path, the old model is rapidly becoming obsolete for many. The old maps don't prepare us well to handle today's quick shifts in the economic and social fabric of our planet.

In describing the natural cycles in the career dynamic, John Caple strengthens our ability to see the opportunities in problematic career situations. New insights allow us to identify the natural condition of our feelings and energy as we move foward—voluntarily or involuntarily—from the domain of security into the realm of versatility and career management.

Careercycles' naturalistic context is not, however, incompatible with practical advice. Several chapters provide important rules for career management where intelligence, energy, and intention interplay with commitment and self-esteem.

Armed with the wisdom of *Careercycles*, a career adventurer can place his or her job at risk and step boldly forth toward a vision that is not simply connected to past history; to try new things, and operate creatively with change.

For those whose lives are about contributing to the work lives of others, and those whose careers are affected by change, this book makes an important contribution.

Tom Jackson

Chairman, The Career Development
Team, Inc., New York

PREFACE

This book is built on a simple idea: that our work life is circular rather than linear. Any idea, to be relevant, must have practical as well as intellectual value, and the central concept described in the pages that follow seems to meet this standard. Those who have worked from the circular perspective have found their work lives becoming more satisfactory.

Careercycles is a guidebook for those who work. Like any useful guidebook, it offers a map to orient the traveler and tells what to expect at each point on that map. It identifies guideposts, both physical and emotional, and it provides specific directions on how to get from one point to another.

A symmetry emerged in the creation of this book. First came twelve chapters and then a title with twelve letters, like the twelve disciples, twelve months in the year, and twelve hours on the face of an analogic clock. Like the clock, this book reflects cycles within cycles: the twelve cycles of the minute hand for each rotation of the hour hand and the many cycles of the hour hand over months and years are not unlike the great and small cycles of life and work described in the pages that follow.

Any errors or omissions in this book are my responsibility, but any luster in what follows must be shared with the many who have helped me along the path. Most particularly I think of:

- Gregory Bateson, who told me, "In fifty years of doing research, I have never *counted* anything."
- Dick Bolles, who has been a marvelous teacher for me in ways neither of us could have anticipated.
- Otto Butz, an academic mentor who led me to see the possibility of this book.
- David Campbell, who showed me the potentials and limitations of testing.
- Joseph Campbell, whose "Hero's Journey" inspired the basic idea in this book.
- Fritjof Capra, who demonstrated that disparate fields of knowledge can be merged into a coherent whole.
- Mary Harper, who taught me about thoroughness and precision in workshop planning.
- Tom Jackson, who proves that pragmatism can be inspiring and inspiration, pragmatic.
- Hal Sarf, whose knowledge of philosophy broadened my understanding of the career cycle.
- The Knights of Lucas Valley Road, Blair Ogden and Harry Scholefield, whose ideas inspried me.
- My father, who taught me the value of work, and my mother, who encouraged me to aspire for the best.
- The San Francisco Foundation and Dominican College, whose financial support contributed mightily to the creation of this book.

The several authorities who read all or part of the manuscript made a number of valuable contributions. Other authors who gave unstintingly of their time and advice helped enormously. Riki Metcalf, an illustrator and former student, was creative and professional in producing the graphic elements in this book. To all, I am grateful.

More than anyone, I am grateful to my wife, Anne, who supported and nourished my dream with patience and enthusiasm through the long gestation period of the pages that follow. This most valuable of friends contributed vignette material, abundant good sense, and extensive editorial and critical comment. For all of this, I am enormously grateful.

My strongest motivation in writing this book was to offer sustenance, knowledge, and inspiration to others, as partial repayment to the many, including those mentioned previously, who have given me these gifts.

Acknowledgment is made to the following for the granting of permission to reprint passages from their publications:

Excerpts from "Little Gidding" and "Burnt Norton" from *Four Quartets* by T. S. Eliot are reprinted by permission of Harcourt Brace Jovanovich, Inc., and Faber & Faber Ltd.; copyright 1943 by T. S. Eliot, renewed 1971 by Esme Valerie Eliot.

The quotation on page 32 is by Albert Camus and is used by permission of Alfred A. Knopf, Inc.

The Freud quotation is from *Childhood and Society* (1950) by Erik Erikson and is used by permission of W. W. Norton and Co., Inc.

The quotation on page 127 is from Philip Roth's *Goodbye Columbus* (copyright © 1959 by Philip Roth) and is reprinted with the permission of Houghton Mifflin Company.

The quotation on page 142 is from Rabindranath Tagore's *Fireflies* (copyright 1928 by Macmillan Publishing Co., Inc., and renewed 1955 by Rabindranath Tagore) and is used by permission of Macmillan Publishing Company and Macmillan Press Ltd.

The quotations on pages 142 and 146 are from *Self-Renewal* by John W. Gardner and are reprinted by permission of The Sterling Lord Agency, Inc. Copyright © 1963 by John W. Gardner.

The quotation on page 147 is from *Motivation and Personality* (Second Ed., 1970) by Abraham Maslow and is used by permission of Harper & Row Publishers Inc.

The quotation from Joseph Campbell on page 152 is from his *The Hero with a Thousand Faces*, Bollingen Series XVII. Copyright 1949 by Princeton University Press. Copyright © renewed 1976 by Princeton University Press.

The quotations by Michael Phillips on pages 166 and 167 are from *The Seven Laws of Money* and are used by permission of Michael Phillips and Random House, Inc.

The quotation on page 219 is from *The Prophet* by Kahlil Gibran and is used by permission of Alfred A. Knopf, Inc. Copyright 1923 by Kahlil Gibran and renewed 1951 by Administrators C.T.A. of Kahlil Gibran Estate, and Mary G. Gibran.

CAREERCYCLES

1

TRADITIONAL
CAREER MAPS:
WHITHER ASCENDING?

Jack and Jill went up the hill
To fetch a pail of water.
Jack fell down and broke his crown
And Jill came tumbling after.

NURSERY RHYME

"The thing I fear most," the poised chief executive was telling me, "is being fired, losing my job." He took another drag on his cigarette. "I have made this job my life."

These seemed like strange words coming from the chairman of a corporation with worldwide sales of over $2 billion, a man whose total reported compensation that year was almost half a million dollars. Yet six months later the board of directors of his company asked for and received this man's resignation. At age fifty-nine he was out, his greatest fear realized.

This is a man who had done it all the right way. He earned an engineering degree and then an MBA from a world-renowned institution. He believes that "success comes from working hard, from being prepared." He got ahead, he told me, by "not ducking the tough things, not being an eight-to-five man." His credo is "Plunge in and produce." Yet after thirty years of moving up the ladder in his company, this executive was unceremoniously dumped.

Although few of us ever work at the top of a giant corporation, most of us at one time or another encounter unpleasant situations at work—including termination. Few of us have the financial resources of the executive described here, so the money impact of losing a job is more severe, more frightening. But regardless of our position, the trauma of a major job change can be enormous. Someone else is in control, a frightening realization. And like Jack in the nursery rhyme, we may bring others down when we fall.

The case of the deposed chief executive raises several questions. What had guided him in his journey to the top? How did his views of his career shape his destiny? What set him up for the fall? And, finally, what can we learn from his experience?

Maps

Early in World War II a battalion of the British Army was forced by Japanese troops to hastily evacuate its base in China and march through the Burmese jungle to safety in India. Three weeks after establishing new headquarters inside the Indian border, one of the British sentries encountered an emaciated, almost naked man staggering out of the jungle. Speaking the King's English, this nomad claimed to be a member of the battalion who had been out of camp when the British escaped China. With only the clothes on his back, he had just made his way to India through 180 miles of inhospitable Burmese jungle.

The British were dubious. This seemed like a classic infiltration attempt by the Japanese. The British commanding officer was convinced that this "survivor" was a spy and, despite prolonged appeals, ordered him sent to the brig.

As the straggler was being taken out of the command tent he made one last attempt to prove his authenticity.

"Wait," he cried, "look at this!" And he pulled from his pocket a tattered map.

The sheet that had gotten this soldier through some of the most primitive jungle in the world proved to be a street map of greater London, cut through by the meandering Thames River. The security of this map—and almost any map would have worked—enabled this dull-witted recruit to achieve his goal through intuition, persistence, and blind luck.

Like the British soldier, we need maps. Like the British soldier, we need reassurance that we are not lost, that we are not alone, and that our actions have meaning. Maps provide guideposts to help us understand where we are in life. And the more accurate the map, the more likely we are to get to where we want to go.

Maps, in the broad sense of the word, help us to organize our experience, to make sense of what is happening. Maps of this kind can provide a context for a diverse and bewildering array of events and emotions. Such maps let us see where we are in life and enable us to go forward with confidence to whatever comes next.

The executive who revealed to me his fears about his job was operating from his own map or set of maps. His views about the work part of his life shaped his behavior and his reactions to what that behavior produced. The same applies to each of us. We have a map or set of maps that guide us through life. These maps indicate to us what we should do at various crossroads and give us a sense of whether we are progressing or falling behind, of whether we are succeeding or failing.

The maps we use make a difference in our lives. The views of life we adopt determine how we act and ultimately how we view the total fabric of our lives. This leads to a central question in living, and in work: Do our maps lead to fulfillment and meaning . . . or to frustration and emptiness?

Traditional Career Maps

In more than one hundred books written before the turn of the century, Horatio Alger wrote about young men achieving success through exemplary living, heroic deeds, and sustained struggle against long odds. Hard work led to big rewards. This view of success, so ingrained in the American psyche, has endured into the twentieth century. When I was working in the world headquarters of the Procter & Gamble Company in the early 1960s, for example, the story of Neil McElroy's rise to the top of the corporation was well established in organizational folklore. *Everyone* knew that McElroy had started with the company as office boy and progressed through the ranks to board chairman, and later secretary of defense under President Eisenhower. All that remained was for each of us to do likewise.

Cream rises to the top, according to traditional maps, even though most of us never get higher than whole milk. How is such ascent measured? A common map charts salary progress (usually in the map reader's mind, since writing down salary figures is considered unseemly). This salary map takes a traditional, linear view of time with past leading to present and on to future. The view of space is also linear, with height as the crucial dimension. Adding the quantitative measure of dollars earned produces a map like that shown in Figure 1.

In Figure 1's map (more accurately, a graph), time moves in just one direction, from left to right, as the years accumulate. Dollars move in two directions: up and down. Salary usually goes up early in life and down later in life, particularly after retirement. Using the graph to chart an individual's progress, it is easy to distinguish the more successful worker from the less successful one by the height of the line.

This map fits a typical college-educated worker who becomes a middle manager in business. Income is low until

FIGURE 1

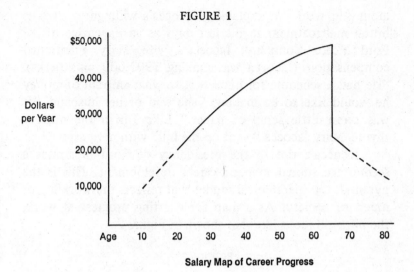

Salary Map of Career Progress

the school years are completed, because part-time jobs pay less, and then grows as promotions come, to some point in the forties. Typically, income then starts to level off. At age sixty-five, this worker retires, and earned income plummets.

Many of us think in these terms—raises every year, at least enough to keep up with inflation, and a tapering off as our value in the competitive market diminishes toward the end of life.

There is plenty of support for readers of salary maps. Newspapers are filled with reports on the latest union settlement for restaurant employees, nurses, and automobile assembly-line workers. A recent book takes more than 700 pages to list salaries for nuclear engineers and radio commentators, store clerks and singers. College alumni publications announce the starting salaries of recent graduates and sometimes those of alumni several years out of school. There is no lack of information to tell us if we are keeping up with Jones, salary-wise.

Lee Iacocca's career illustrates the symbolic role of

money in work. In explaining Iacocca's willingness to take brutal maltreatment in his last days as an executive of the Ford Motor Company, Iacocca's wife, Mary, mentioned compensation (Iacocca was making $901,000 plus perks). "He had a schedule for himself as to what amount of money he would like to be making," she said of her husband. "It was on a little scrap of paper." Like Jill in the nursery rhyme, Mary Iacocca "went up the hill" with her partner.

Iacocca's rise to the presidency of Ford illustrates a second traditional map of career development. This is the pyramid, the hierarchical model that reflects the workings of much of society. As a map for charting progress at work, the pyramid looks like that shown in Figure 2.

FIGURE 2

Pyramidal Map of Career Progress

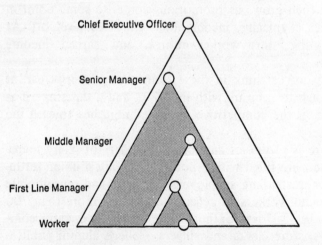

In this model, there are really only two directions for movement: up and down. Like the childhood game "King of the mountain, " only one can stay at the top, and getting there usually involves pulling someone else down.

In the hierarchical model, a college-educated worker starts at the bottom, and after demonstrating merit, becomes a first-line manager. This worker, if the American dream is operating, becomes a middle manager, senior manager, and finally, at age fifty or fifty-five, emerges at the top in the rarified atmosphere of the chief executive officer. This executive has succeeded, where others have "failed."

Unfortunately, maps like those charting income and progress up the pyramid have major flaws.

How Traditional Maps Mislead

Perhaps the major weakness of traditional maps is that they largely ignore the value of change. By measuring progress only in terms of salary growth or increased responsibility, these traditional views fail to acknowledge the joy, excitement, and human growth that come when we create change in our work life.

The vulnerabilities of the American view emerge when the Japanese approach to managing people is examined. Although the Japanese are more likely to stay with one company for a working lifetime, they are also more likely to encounter a great deal of change within that company, with transfers from marketing to accounting to the factory floor not unusual. The position with the highest status in a Japanese company is the personnel department, where employees become involved with assisting others in assignment changes.

A second weakness of traditional American views of career development is the emphasis on growth. Growth is the goal, and the faster the better, according to the conventional wisdom. Move up at the maximum rate in compensation and position and you are on course, according to the traditional maps. Never mind that continuing growth can be deadly for some.

Growth is a pervasive organizational ideal, as exemplified by increasing concentration in business. Yet maximum growth is a relatively new idea, certainly at odds with the golden mean of the ancient Greeks. We may *choose* to stay in a job that is right for us rather than agitate for a promotion. We may settle for the money we need and seek to maximize value in our lives rather than value in our pocketbooks.

Traditional maps glorify the god *maxima* despite the mounting evidence that *optima* is a more appropriate deity and should once again be given reverence. Optimal career development recognizes nonquantitative factors. Optimal growth incorporates the human dimension. Optimal progress makes sense on a planet shared by many.

A third weakness of traditional maps is that ultimately they guide only the few. Those at the top of income graphs or organizational hierarchies are an elite, a small minority composed mainly of older caucasian males. For the rest there is frustration or the unsettling prospect of abandoning the common values reflected in traditional maps. The focus in the traditional view is *exclusivity*, rather than *inclusivity*. Traditional maps leave people out, rather than draw people in. Traditional maps are for the few, not the many.

A fourth weakness of the two traditional maps described in this chapter is that in neither is there a connection between the starting point and the finishing point. The beginning comes out of nowhere and tapers off into nowhere. Even the road map we use to help us drive from New York to San Francisco shows us many ways to get back.

Is it possible that the traditional maps have contributed to our widely felt sense of disconnectedness between work and the rest of life? Could it be that the sense of alienation felt by many who work is related to the maps that have traditionally guided our perceptions of work? There must be a better way.

A final flaw in the traditional maps is that they set us up for the inevitable fall that comes after ascension. They show us the way to the top and leave us there. As any mountain climber knows, "What goes up, must come down." Both the salary graph and pyramidal map assume upward progress and leave us on our own for the inevitable decline.

Rise and then fall is the stuff of tragedy. Consider *Oedipus Rex* or *Othello* or the human tragedies shouted out daily in the news. Fall and then rise is the stuff of comedies. Consider *A Midsummer's Night Dream* or Laurel and Hardy or the jokes we most enjoy. Life includes *both* tragedy and comedy.

As counterbalance to the Horatio Alger stories of the American dream, consider the novels of Theodore Dreiser. A tale like *Sister Carrie*, published in 1900, pictures the business hero, Hurstwood, arrived at the top of the pyramid as president of a Chicago bank. But the story goes on to show Hurstwood's fall as he loses family, friends, and fortune. At the story's end Hurstwood dies in a Bowery flophouse, unknown and penniless. Our maps prepare us for the ascent but how much do they help on the descent? Must they fail us then?

On a Monday morning in 1975, the chief executive officer of United Brands was dropped by his chauffeur at the 245 Park Avenue world headquarters of his corporation, took the elevator to the forty-fourth floor, entered his sumptuous office, smashed out a window with his briefcase, and jumped to his death. The tragedy of Eli Black reflects much that is wrong with traditional views of career development.

Another board chairman, who had talked with Black a few months earlier, told me:

> We met at a business conference in Brussels and I was surprised at how angry and hostile he was. It jumped out at you. He was not the kind of guy you'd want to be around.

Little wonder! Black had followed the accepted career maps to the top and now found his position unstable and himself frustrated and unfulfilled. With no map to guide him, with no sense of a meaningful future, this sad man took the only path he could see.

Existing maps have some worth, certainly, and they incorporate attitudes that many of us share. As the British soldier struggling through the Burmese jungle discovered, some map is better than none at all. But the gnawing question remains: Can we somehow sharpen our focus on reality and improve the guidelines for our work life? Is there a better map?

Because current maps for career growth are flawed and inaccurate, it is essential to explore other views. In the next chapter an alternative perspective, a new map, unfolds.

2

A NEW MAP:
THE HERO'S JOURNEY
AND CAREERCYCLES

We shall not cease from exploration
And the end of all our exploring,
Will be to arrive where we started
And know the place for the first time.

T. S. ELIOT

To every thing there is a season,
and a time for every purpose under the
heaven: a time to be born and a time
to die; a time to plant and a time to
reap; a time to kill and a time to heal;
a time to break down and a time
to build up.

ECCLESIASTES 3:1-3

"I hope there's reincarnation," the chief executive of one of California's half-dozen largest employers was telling me. "I would accomplish more the second time around. I would stay away from the corporate world next time. . . . I might even be a farmer."

Eastern views on afterlife are hardly what one expects to hear in the executive suite, and this articulate manager later told me that he is a practicing Episcopalian. Yet his idea about going around again clearly anticipates the map drawn in this chapter. More to the point, this executive's life reflects a career map that works.

Like the executive described at the start of the first chapter, the manager who hopes there is reincarnation left his company within a year of our meeting. But the first was asked to resign, and the would-be farmer chose early retirement. Both were facing declining profits, both were under lots of pressure, and both might have stayed on to normal retirement age if results had been better in the companies they managed. The first executive found that his job was his life, but the second executive anticipated with obvious gusto getting more involved in an organization he had founded to "get third and fourth generation welfare people working again." And he hoped to find more time for golf, an avocation since his college days as a national champion.

What can we learn from the lives of these executives?

The Hero's Journey

In seeking direction in our lives, we can look for inspiration from the examples of others. Looking back helps us to move ahead. The executive preparing for new challenges, for instance, still remembered studying the great books twenty years earlier with Mortimer Adler. The myths that have shaped civilized culture contain some of the answers to twentieth-century dilemmas.

Mythology is the basis for a map of the Hero's Journey, which offers promise here. This was described by Joseph Campbell in *The Hero with a Thousand Faces* as a circular map, as shown in Figure 3.

The journey summarized in this diagram starts with a call to adventure. The hero (and Campbell would add now, heroine) responds to this lure, often with the support of a helper. At the threshhold of adventure, the hero often traverses a guarded passageway. Beyond the threshhold the hero encounters forces that threaten him, in the form of tests, or forces that give magical aid, in the form of helpers. At the bottom of the cycle, the hero undergoes the supreme ordeal and wins his reward. The hero then begins his return, possibly with the protection of the forces he has encountered or, if these powers are unfriendly, in flight. When the hero is at the threshhold again, the transcendental powers must remain behind but he brings across an elixir, the boon that restores the world.

FIGURE 3

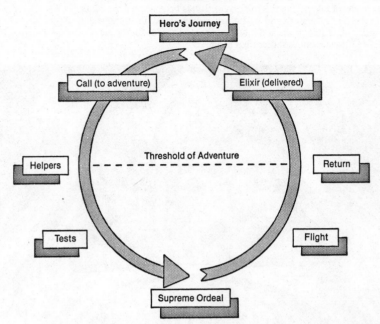

The stories of heroes like Odysseus or Jonah illustrate this map, but one of the most relevant tales for our purposes, particularly as illustrated in the etchings of William Blake (Figure 4), is that of the Old Testament figure Job.

Job is "the greatest of all the men of the east" at the start of the story. Job has prestige, possessions, family. Everything seems fine with Job, just as things often seem fine with us just before the start of an adventure.

Then messengers come to Job to report the loss of his oxen, sheep, asses, and camels and finally to report the death of his sons and daughters. Job is getting a message, a call to adventure disguised as bad news. In our work life we also get such messages, indicating that conditions are changing. And although these messages are disconcerting, the sooner they are viewed as a call to adventure, the sooner we can begin to start our journey.

FIGURE 4. In this 1825 etching by William Blake (one of twenty-one in a series depicting the Job myth), Job is being shown the biblical monsters Behemoth and Leviathon. Having faced his supreme ordeal, Job is able to see and integrate these powerful forces and relate to them as allies rather than enemies.

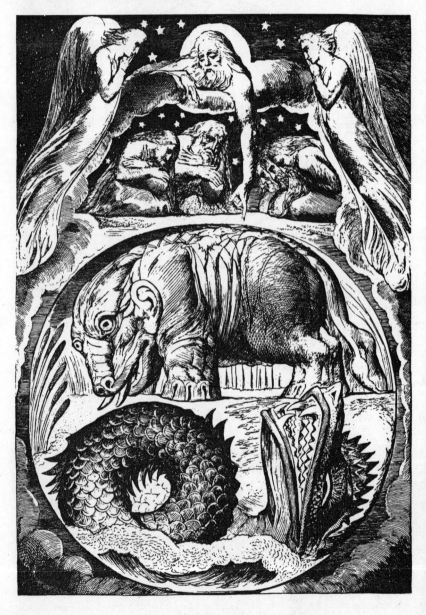

Job had a helper on his journey, a figure Job viewed as trouble, in the form of Satan who "smote Job with sore boils." Job is now forced to pay attention, compelled to consider change. Our helpers may also appear as trouble, perhaps in the form of a decline in the demand for the kind of work we do or in the guise of a hostile supervisor. When we, like Job, feel the impact of this "help," we are getting prepared for adventure.

"After this, Job opened his mouth." Finally Job acts. For Job, this response is a commitment to action, a decision to come alive in the face of adversity. Job crosses the threshold of adventure. In the process of human change, including career change, there also comes the crucial moment of action, the moment of no turning back. This can be an internal shift, a spoken decision, or a significant action. Whatever form it takes, we *know* the moment, for here our adventure begins in earnest.

Job faces tests. As he proceeds, he declares that "man is born into trouble," and certainly that is Job's perception. Likewise, when we change we face tests, challenges to our ingenuity and resourcefulness. We are rejected, often more than once, and forced to seek again, perhaps in different directions, the path for our change.

More helpers for Job come in the form of three friends: Eliphaz, Bildad, and Zophar. The three friends tell Job that his problems are God's will. "Is not thy wickedness great?" asks Eliphaz, suggesting that Job is getting what he deserves. Our helpers may likewise be naysayers, people close to us engrossed with their own fears about the possibility for change they see in us. Or our helpers may be guides who see where we are going because they have been there themselves, and support us and guide us in our journey. Both kinds of helpers are important.

At some point it becomes clear that Job has gained a deeper wisdom, a new and special view of the world. "I am a brother to dragons and a companion to owls," Job cries, and it is clear that he is changed. In our journey the payoff is usually wisdom, a new view of reality, and it may be a job opportunity that we never imagined we could have. Whatever its nature, we *know* we have achieved the prize.

The start of Job's return journey is symbolized by the appearance of the young Elihu, who tells Job to "stand up!" For us this may be the point where we begin to integrate new-found wisdom or when we accept a newly offered job, perhaps in a new career. The feeling is one of escape, of relief at leaving the intensity of the challenge for calmer moments ahead.

As Job recrosses the threshhold of adventure he tells God, "I have heard of thee by the hearing of the ear; but now mine eye seeth thee." The elixir Job brings back is expanded power and aliveness. He has vision. For us also the completion of the crossover is a time of power. Job faced "the thing which I greatly feared" and returned, and we do likewise. And the power that flows from our success is an elixir, a boon and an inspiration to others, a gift of the highest quality. We are closer to becoming all that we can be.

"So the Lord blessed the latter end of Job more than his beginning," the story concludes. At the end, "the Lord gave Job twice as much as he had before," including his sons and daughters, whom Job thought were lost. Job ends up more enriched and more fully human than when the journey began. Job's risks and pain are rewarded, as ours are.

Job thus completes the cycle. His journey takes him to the points described in the diagram at the start of this chapter, the full circle. This is the Hero's Journey, the venture into uncertainty taken by Dante, Odysseus, Jonah, Jason, and many others. And it is available to us.

But is the circular map of the Hero's Journey really a meaningful way to understand career growth?

Why a Circular Map?

Consider first the nature of the circle.

If we progress far enough on a circle we come back to where we started. This result is inherent in a shape that has neither beginning nor end. This is also a phenomenon found repeatedly in nature. Some twenty-four hours after dawn we come back to where we started—dawn. About twenty-eight days after the full moon, we arrive again at the same point. Some 365 days after one winter solstice, there arrives another.

The moon, itself a three-dimensional circle, turns in a circular orbit around planet earth. The earth, another three-dimensional circle, rotates in a circular path as it moves in a circular orbit around the sun. Other planets circle the sun also. And it seems likely that a similar pattern acts in other solar systems, making the circle a universal pattern, a map for the entire cosmos.

Although it is true that nature is full of circles, it is also true that nature contains change. From one dawn to another, profound change can occur. From one full moon to another or from one winter solstice to another there can be massive changes in life forms or geology. Each dawn, each new moon is like what T. S. Eliot calls "the unknown remembered gate." We return to the same place, yet it is different.

Nature, then, incorporates *both* cycles and change. So does the map of the Hero's Journey described earlier.

Human existence, too, unfolds in cycles. Those who study biorhythms tell us that life is a series of cycles. There seems to be a human cycle that corresponds to the twenty-four-hour cycle of the sun, with high points and low points, awake times and asleep times. And there are longer high and low cycles, some three or four days between peaks, some twenty-five or thirty days, some lasting months or years. In work life there are cycles of a few months ranging upward to many years. One top executive I interviewed, for instance, has "repotted" himself every ten years in careers involving both business management and academic administration.

Life ultimately can be viewed as a large cycle in which we are powerless and simple at both the beginning and the end. As infants we are toothless, weak, and inchoate, and many human beings complete their lives this same way. We arrive where we started "and know the place for the first time."

Is the idea of life cycles new? The Hero's Journey was first described in 1949, but thinkers for centuries have seen life as circular. Buddhism, for instance, teaches about the wheel of life, and Jainism sees time as an endless round, a wheel with twelve spokes, or ages. American Indian shamans taught a medicine wheel with four positions in the human journey. For these people and others the circle, or *mandala*, is a symbol of wholeness, representing the complete person.

The philosopher Nietzsche wrote of eternal recurrence in his theory of ultimate reality, creating a circular view of life from another perspective. For Nietzsche, nothing is lost and nothing is gained—reality is continually being rediscovered.

Nor is the circle new for career applications. In 1973, John Holland wrote about a theory of careers and identified six groupings based on interests: realistic, investigative, artistic, social, enterprising, and conventional. These he presented graphically as a hexagon, circular in appearance.

A circular map has several advantages over linear models like the salary graph and management pyramid described in the first chapter:

- The circular model better allows for human growth by including downward movement as well as upward movement.
- The circular model is one of optimization rather than maximization because there is no single apex for all to aim at.

- In the circular model there is a natural connection between beginning and end (more accurately, there *is* no beginning and there is no end).
- The circular model incorporates comedy (fall and then rise) in addition to tragedy (rise and then fall) since both are described and one is considered as valuable as the other. On the journey of life, we encounter *both* triumph and disaster.

The Hero's Journey, then, which can be viewed as circular in nature, may provide a useful way to understand changes in work life.

A New Map

Can a circular map be relevant for organizing career change? If so, what can the career changer expect at various points in the journey?

There seem to be at least six discernable steps in the career change process, that can be mapped as shown in Figure 5.

With this map a typical member of the workforce, perhaps early in life, might feel some dissatisfaction with the established routine. This worker would explore options, often through interviews with other employers. At about this point the worker commits—to a course of action, to a new career, to a particular organization—and this leads to change. Then comes renewal, with the excitement of a new and stimulating environment. As the months wear on, the worker consolidates skills and interests, and grows in mastery over the work being done. This is followed by recommitment to work, to achieving the goals in the job, and possibly to future job changes.

When this first cycle has been completed, generally in two to five years, the worker comes again to the discontent phase and is ready for further exploration. Most typically

FIGURE 5

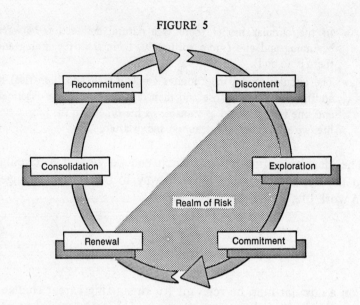

this is a more challenging assignment in the same organization, though it can be a job elsewhere or, more rarely, a new career. The cycle is then repeated, perhaps several times in the course of a life.

Reflecting the passage of time, this cycle moves in a clockwise direction, contrary to the Hero's Journey (Joseph Campbell wrote me that in the Hero's Journey "the quest involves a *return to source*, hence the counterclockwise way"). In the careercycle the "threshhold of adventure" is replaced by the "realm of risk," starting late in the discontent stage. This is not to say that this round is not an adventure, but rather that risk is more descriptive of the environment in which work decisions are made.

The points on this new map deserve explanation.

Discontent is the start of the cycle, the energy that gets us moving. This is a dissatisfaction with the way things are, usually a mild malaise. It is the divine discontent that drives geniuses and makes itself felt from time to time in all of us.

Discontent can be an inner state, a gnawing feeling that something is not right, or it can appear to come from our environment—a change in conditions, rejections from those we serve, a boss turned hostile. Whatever the perceived source of our discontent, it is usually some *combination* of the inner and the outer.

Discontent can also have either a negative or positive form. The negative stimuli, often from our environment, tell us that we are not doing well enough. These signals shoot directly at the ego and can be acutely painful. Positive stimuli are less intense and are usually perceived as coming from within, or from our own value system. These messages raise the question: Can I do better? As with inner and outer sources of discontent, negative and positive usually work in tandem. The overall impact is some *combination* of negative and positive.

If we get stuck somewhere on this circular map, and most of us do at some time or another, the discontent stage is where it is likely to happen. We decide, like Job, that life is meant to be painful. Being "courageous," we grit our teeth and muddle through. What happens then is that we are stuck, immobilized. We decide that we prefer the devil we know to the devil we don't know. Often it takes an enormous amount of discontent to get us rolling. Or someone may act from the outside with the words "You're fired!" and this may be far more fortuitous than we appreciate at the time. For if we continue to ignore the messages of discontent, the result is stagnation, frustration, depression, rage, suicide.

Exploration flows from discontent. This stage marks the transition from a passive to an active posture. Exploration is extending ourselves out into our environment, sending out scouting parties, testing, evaluating, seeking, searching.

Exploration can take many forms. We can launch an inner investigation, often extensive, looking at our experiences, feelings, impulses—our whole work history and value system. We can speak out: talk to family, friends, others who are doing work we feel attracted to. We can mount an active search for information, scheduling interviews with those working in areas we would like to investigate. We can go beyond this to test out kinds of work we think we would enjoy by getting a weekend volunteer job, writing an article, or teaching a course at a local church or junior college. Or we can go even further and take the steps necessary to be offered a full-time job, giving ourselves a major new option.

The famous explorers of this country—from Lewis and Clark to Admiral Byrd—traversed vast, uncharted areas of the globe. As we explore, we, too, traverse uncharted areas and we, too, travel the road to discovery and adventure.

Commitment develops from exploration. Once the explorer has enough data, enough answers, the commitment is made. Commitment comes from making a decision. In the process described here, the decision is to loose the moorings from the past and set sail for a new and different future, still not fully known. We *know* when we commit. Unlike some of the other stages in this circular journey, commitment is clear and precise and happens at a single point in time. It is like a switch going from "off" to "on." There is no uncertainty.

The root word of *commitment* is *mittere*, the Latin verb meaning "to send." So although the idea has a sense of finality, it also has a sense of movement, of process. Commitment is also an idea of power, of focused energy. Commitment commands respect. As the first president of Stanford University, David Starr Jordan, said, "The world stands aside for the man who knows where he's going."

Somewhere after commitment and before renewal the high magic of this whole process occurs. It is different each time for each of us, but the common element is that change happens. We are never the same again. For the hero, the nadir of the mythological round occurs when he undergoes a supreme ordeal and gains his reward—like Job. With careers it is the same, though the ordeal may be the stress of the final job interviews and the reward may be the offer we have sought. We feel the enormous emotional relief from the intensity built up during the pursuit of a goal, almost as though we had been holding our breath and could finally let go. The immediate aftermath is euphoria, and a tremendous sense of well-being.

Renewal builds from this sense of well-being and rediscovered confidence. Although in some ways this entire circular journey is invigorating, the renewal phase in particular is marked by the arrival of new power, new energy, new life force. The traveler is restored to freshness and vigor in what is almost a spiritual regeneration. The source of this personal renaissance is the aliveness regained through commitment and engaging our own supreme ordeal. Renewal is the career changer's first realization that he or she has become the possessor of a boon or elixir of enormous power. This awareness is like the joy of a child in the first moments with a long-awaited toy.

Renewal is also the recognition that we *can* rearrange our lives, that we *are* successful persons. We have faced the challenge, like a hero, and we come away intoxicated with the delight of our achievement.

Have you ever been with someone just back from a marvelous vacation? Have you ever listened to a friend just returned from a weekend that "changed my life"? As passive observers, without the shared experience, we can find this buoyancy obnoxious. Yet there is no mistaking the power produced by change. This power comes from renewal.

Renewal, like all emotionally altered states, like all highs, cannot last. Before long this new energy is integrated into a consolidation phase.

Consolidation is the process of coming back into reality as we cross the threshhold of adventure and enter a more stable territory. The core word of consolidate is *solidare*, the Latin verb meaning "to make firm." This period of consolidation is a time for firming up, for solidifying the diverse energies generated by change and renewal.

For the career changer, consolidation is a time to savor victory while using newfound energy to master new challenges. A new broom sweeps clean, according to the aphorism, and the worker in the new job brings new energy and creativity to the learning process involved. This is a honeymoon phase, a period of high interest and rare boredom.

In the learning process the career changer becomes aware of new joys at work—some anticipated and some not—and also some of the old problems. The worker can see the truth in the old saw that "The more things change, the more they stay the same." As such sobering insights emerge, the traveler becomes ready for the next phase, recommitment.

Recommitment, the sixth and final phase in this circular sequence, involves acknowledging completion of the process and dedicating ourselves, perhaps even resigning ourselves, to repeating the full cycle. Recommitment requires a willingness to continue learning, the courage to once again venture into uncharted territory.

"Once you leave Wonderland," the Cheshire cat said to Alice, "you can never go back." Once we have been through the cycle described here—with the awareness that it *is* a journey—the cycle will never again have quite the same wonder, and certainly not the same terrors. Recommitment is a conscious decision to go there again, to once again venture after the elixir.

Recommitment brings us back to the top of the cycle, to the point where the seeds of discontent may once again take root. As Eliot says, "we arrive where we started, and know the place for the first time." Once again we enter into the sequence of *discontent*, *exploration*, *commitment*, *renewal*, *consolidation*, and *recommitment*, but now with a new alertness.

How does this work in the real world? Here are the

words from a man I'll call Bill, a man whose career I have helped manage in recent months:

> I first got into police work because I needed income while going to school. There was a cadet program in the police department where you worked twenty hours a week. I became mesmerized.
>
> During my nine years in the force I had a lot of dynamic things going on. I worked in the car, under cover, as a body guard to superiors, and later to the mayor.
>
> I was one of the first police officers on high school campuses at a time when there was lots of gang violence and killing. We eliminated all that and then they withdrew the funding and a week later two kids got killed.
>
> I was becoming more and more disenchanted. Court decisions at that time made life tough and it was hard with my background to be competitive for promotion (as a white, straight male). I went back to college part time and at the same time was assigned to teach report writing at the police academy.
>
> I did a resume and sent it to nine or ten companies, all major companies. I took a $3000 pay cut to take a job in facilities management in industry.
>
> It was absolutely horrible in the beginning. For one thing I had been deceitful with my wife. I had quit the police force—I felt I had to—but I told my wife I was on leave. Then at work I was thrown in with senior management people and was somewhat intimidated by the corporate power structure.
>
> Thirty days into the new job I was given a project with six months to complete it. That was my goal. If I succeed in this, I'm over the hump. I can do anything.
>
> I would never have gone back. I would have pounded nails, pumped gas, anything.

I'm still very much on a high. It's still going and hasn't stopped yet. I see myself as very dynamic and very adaptive. I think I underestimated myself for a number of years.

Where's the next ball? I don't want to get entrenched. My next career change will be less radical. I will be more selective. I want to get more into marketing and sales. I want more people involvement.

I'm still fulfilling my dream.

Can you follow Bill's journey along the cycle? Police work was good, and then *discontent* started to develop. Bill began *exploring* by returning to school and then sending out resumes. For Bill, *commitment* was resigning from the police force and his supreme ordeal came during the "absolutely horrible" first weeks in industry. Two years later he is still "very much on a high" with *renewal* but has started to *consolidate* his position. He is now secure enough to *recommit* to continued career growth, perhaps in "sales and marketing" and probably in the same company.

In the sixteenth century the Flemish geographer Mercator created a map using parallel meridians, building on the second-century maps of Ptolemy in Alexandria. In the same way, traditional maps of career growth provide a foundation for creating a new map. Each place on this new map needs to be described, with sufficient detail for the inexperienced traveler to find the way. Further, the map unfolding here offers suggestions to the traveler on how to get to whatever destination is chosen next. We start, in the next chapter, with discontent.

3

DISCONTENT:
FUEL FOR
THE JOURNEY

Without work all life goes rotten.
But when work is soulless,
Life stifles and dies.

ALBERT CAMUS

The heart has its reasons
Reason can not know.

BLAISE PASCAL

"I dread going into the classroom each morning," the third grade teacher told me. "Those kids are demanding, unruly, disrespectful."

"I went into teaching twenty years ago," she continued. "The schools were clamoring for *any* college graduate and it seemed like a good job.

"I had thought a little about doing scientific research, maybe for a big company, but now . . ." She turned wistful. "I was divorced five years ago and I need every nickel of my teaching salary to support my son and me. And next year he goes to college.

"I really hate what I'm doing, but I don't see any way to change without totally ruining my life," she concluded.

Discontent. We all have some of it and at times it can seem overpowering. The workshop participant whose words are paraphrased above felt overwhelmed by a continuing discontent with her work, a malaise from which she saw no escape. In this chapter we will examine both positive and negative faces of discontent. We will look at discontent that comes from within and that which mainly originates outside us. We will consider ways to identify and understand discontent. And toward the end of the chapter, we will start to see ways discontent can become a force for positive change in our lives.

Discontent comes from the Latin word *continere* meaning "to hold together, restrain." Thus discontent literally means "falling apart, unrestrained." Discontent is clearly a signal for imminent change, dissatisfaction crying to be heard.

Discontent is motivation. The greater our discontent, the greater our motivation. As the force which drives geniuses, it is called divine discontent. It is what motivated Marco Polo to leave Venice and explore the East for seventeen years. It is what drove Winston Churchill to come back from crushing defeat to lead Britain's fight against the Axis in World War II. Each of us experiences discontent at different periods with different intensities. The questions we face are: How can we identify discontent? How can we make sense of it? How can we use it?

The starting point is inner discontent.

Inner Discontent

The articulate, attractive, candid president of a major retailing chain recently told me the following story:

> When I was sixteen I played on an all-black baseball team in the Bronx. Well, almost all black. I played third base and was the lead-off batter. We had a terrific team and made it to the championships and for the first time ever, my father came to see me play.

I was this skinny white kid who usually got singles and in this game I was getting doubles and triples. In the field I made impossible catches. My teammates even commented on my amazing play. At the end of the sixth inning my father left the stands and never, *ever* said a word to me about the game.

My older sister was very bright. She was always looking for that pat on the back. What I learned from that experience at age sixteen was that I could never, ever jump high enough to get that myself. *Nobody* is going to give you the pat on the back you crave.

One way of understanding discontent is that it springs from unmet needs. The executive telling the baseball story still feels a need for his father's love, for his father's acceptance. And that still-felt need continues to be a driving force for this intense and perceptive man.

Discontent can also be seen as unmet expectations. With unmet expectations there is a widening gap between what we expect and what we perceive as reality. At some point the gulf grows to where the discontent is felt and perhaps identified for what it is. Our expectations come from our needs and from our values and when the gap gets too great, the pain can grow intense.

Ultimately we must deal with the expectation that there should be meaning in life.

The pull to meaning is a form of positive discontent, an itch that impels us to move ahead. The feeling expressed in the song lyric "Is that all there is?" is a kind of positive discontent. It is motivation to seek more, to find our role in life, to become the best that we can become.

Negative discontent, by contrast, is more push than pull. The pain and unhappiness mount until we decide that we can stand no more. So we act. Positive and negative discontent may intermingle in the same life issue. They may mix with one another as our perceptions vary from moment to moment. Both the positive and negative energies of discontent have the potential to motivate us, and both must be responded to if we hope for wholeness and richness in our lives.

Signs of Discontent

"Big boys don't cry," we are told. Or "Big girls don't cry." There is lots of pressure from parents, siblings, peers, society to ignore discontent, to ignore pain. "Life isn't perfect," we are reminded, or, in the words of a recent President, "Life isn't fair." The message is that a little suffering is good for us. It comes with the territory. So don't give in to it and perhaps when you grow up into a mature adult you will learn to ignore such signals. Or so goes the conventional wisdom.

Is it little wonder, then, that we have a hard time understanding our discontent? And are reluctant to respond to it?

Remember the old cartoon where the man comes home from a rough day at the office and kicks the dog? One way to understand such behavior is to call it displaced anger. But in the career cycle, it might also be a sign of discontent not identified. The dog is not responsible for unhappiness at work yet, in the moment, our unexpressed discontent pours out on our pet. Part of making our discontent work *for* us is to correctly identify its nature and its source.

What are some signals of discontent?

While discontent affects the entire human organism that is us, signals may first be received on one or the other of the main levels on which we live: physical, mental, emotional, or intuitive. This four-dimensional view of persons was taught by the Swiss psychologist Carl Jung and provides a helpful way for sorting out discontent.

Physical discontent affects the body. Somewhere we hurt and the pain is right now, sometimes grabbing our attention to the exclusion of all else. Whole books have been written on stress and its effects, both negative and positive. Stress, and the tension that accompanies it, seem to be the source points for discontent signaled to us through our bodies. And although Americans take millions of pills daily to blot out such messages, the messages still come through.

Back pain and belly pain are two of the most common body signals. Muscle spasms in the back, a back "gone out," even the diagnosis of a disintegrating disc in the back *may* be telling us something. A close friend of mine can relate stress and concerns in her life to each of the three times her back caused her severe pain; in her mind the cause and effect relationship is direct and clear. Likewise with belly pain. Most of us can recall the physical feeling of tightness in our abdomen, our stomach "tied up in knots." Many of us have had this experience at work. Early in my business career I worked with an experienced, wise sales executive who used to talk about the trauma of reporting directly to the demanding founder of the company that employed us both. "Abey, Benny, and Charlie" were his momentos from the experience, three ulcers, which healed when my friend got a new and less fearsome boss.

Is it purely coincidence that both of these common pain areas are in the part of the body associated in Eastern religions with power? The third *chakra*, or energy center, is considered the locus of power motivation in the body and is located roughly at the navel in the region of both the sacroiliac and the belly (the big belly on statues of the Buddha symbolizes power). Given the values in our society, it seems probable that much discontent at work springs from power struggles.

One caveat on physical pain. I am *not* saying that all physical pain is caused by discontent or stress. There is much about the body that even the most advanced medical scientists do not know. Much of the pain and disease in our bodies appear to come from purely organic causes unrelated to outside forces. Some physical problems are inherited. And yet if we view ourselves as complex and integrated systems we can at least *consider* causes beyond the purely physical when pain strikes.

Psychological discontent affects the emotions. The root word of *psychological* is *psyche*, which means "the soul" in Greek—and discontent of the soul is certainly relevant here. What are the emotions of work? Ideally, joy, satisfaction, fulfillment, even love. But we also know that frustration, anger, hopelessness, and depression can be emotions of work. These powerful signals of discontent call out the need for change.

Several years ago the founder of a national direct sales company told me a story pregnant with the emotions of the workplace. This company owner had brought in a long-time friend to be president. Things had not worked out and, after increasing pressure from the board, the decision was made to ask for the president's resignation. The founder of the company, hoping to soften the blow, spoke candidly to his friend on the Friday before the Monday board meeting in which the axe was to fall. On Sunday, the friend committed suicide.

The emotional impact of this on the company founder was enormous and, I felt sure, a major reason why he was no longer active in managing his company. The greatest tragedy, of course, is that the company president could see only one alternative to dealing with his overwhelming emotional pain. That same energy turned toward life—discontent transformed into commitment—could have had an enormous impact.

Stimuli that affect the emotions are processed through the mind at one point or another so that the mental and emotional dimensions are inextricably intertwined.

Mental discontent affects our thoughts. This is our conscious mind, our logical, computing function, the left brain. Our mind processes information like "this is a good job" or, after a bad experience, "this job is terrible!" We evaluate and assess. We compare ourselves with co-workers, with what our father or mother did, with what our value system indicates we *should* be doing.

In dealing with satisfaction and discontent the mind does a balancing act. Written down, such an analysis might look like this:

Sources of Satisfaction	Sources of Discontent
Good money	Boring work
Easy commute	Long hours
Friendly co-workers	Insensitive boss
Ample benefits	Limited vacation

This kind of exercise can be helpful, as we shall see in the next chapter, or it can lead to debilitating rationalizations. Used in this sense, rationalizations occur when we create reasons for liking something we really don't. Listen to Maryann, whose career I have helped manage:

> I had a job for six years where for most of that time I was very bored. The people there were boring. I died a thousand deaths. I was miserable and I cried a lot.
>
> But I had good rapport with my boss. I talked with him about government, the world, my marriage, things I couldn't talk about with my husband or anyone else at that time.
>
> I didn't have the confidence that I could do anything else. So stupid!

Although there was a lot going on with Maryann at this point in her career, one piece of it was her rationalization: "I'm bored with this job *but* I have this wonderful relationship with my boss *and* I probably couldn't get anything better anyway." Her mind took discontent and, through an elaborate balancing act, concluded that it was not such a big deal.

More than any other locus, the mind deals with ethical issues that cause discontent at work. Ethical decision making involves balancing altruism with practical considerations and the scale reads differently for each of us. Ethical decisions are made on issues ranging from pollution control to nuclear energy, from consumerism to discrimination in hiring.

Ethical issues can be quite personal. A young man might choose not to work for a wine distributor because of his feelings about his alcoholic father. A woman manager's feminist beliefs might dissuade her from working for a traditional manufacturer that has no female vice presidents or directors. We all must decide by our own lights. To paraphrase an old cliché: "In your heart you know when it's wrong." Violating what we know in our heart causes discontent.

Part of what we know in our heart comes through mental processes. And part comes through intuitive channels. As Pascal said, "The heart has its reasons. . . ."

Intuitive discontent affects our spirit. Intuitive signals are the hardest to catch and the easiest to ignore—yet they may be the most honest and the most important. Intuitive is a sense we have, a hunch. Once, after a long and arduous search, a company I worked for was about to hire a district sales manager for Southern California. The top applicant had an excellent background, great experience, and fine recommendations, but as several of us walked to lunch a couple of hours before the job offer was formally made, I had a sense that something was wrong. He walked funny. I even commented on it. Within a year this prime candidate was fired for dishonesty; it turned out that in addition to being light on his feet, this man was too easy with facts and with company funds. From that point on I trusted my intuition more, both in making employment decisions and as part of my own process.

Intuitive messages often come from our unconscious mind, the part that is normally inaccessible to us. They can come to us as a hunch, as in the story above, or they may come to us while we are sleeping in the form of a dream. Some people are especially inclined to have precognitive dreams, dreams in which they see the future. Toward the end of a nap recently I dreamed that I was opening the evening newspaper and saw a photograph of my son high-jumping. An hour later, though I don't consider myself particularly intuitive, I saw the actual picture in the paper and found it quite similar to the one in my dream. Discontent at work may appear in our dreams—it certainly has for me—and if we pay close attention we may be able to understand, and even act upon, such messages.

The observant reader will have noticed that the four categories described above—physical, mental, emotional, and intuitive—overlap considerably. It is convenient to talk about these four dimensions of humanness separately but it is important not to forget that the four are in fact integrated and intermingled.

Explaining the four dimensions is a little like describing a horse to a being from outer space. We could talk about the parts of the horse to begin to create a picture of the whole. We could describe the appearance and functions of the various parts. But we would need to remember that a leg and a tail, though seemingly separate in nature and function, are in fact interrelated and work together as integral parts of the whole horse. Likewise with the parts and the sum of human beings.

Much of the inner discontent described above can be traced to issues of power. Power, defined simply, is the capacity to cause change. Physical power as measured, say, by how many pounds we can lift, is relevant at work when women apply for jobs traditionally held by men. Judging by the number of women taking such employment, this kind of power is rarely critical to job success.

More relevant than physical power in most work situations, however, is psychological power, the subjective ability to control other human beings. This is the kind of power we feel in our gut. This is the kind of power that tears at our emotions. This is the kind of power that works itself out in our dreams.

In a very real sense this book is about power. Each of us needs the capacity to cause change in our lives, and particularly in the work part of our lives. Understanding where we are, where we want to go, and how we might get there are the first steps to claiming our power. Knowledge is power. Action is power. If this book works, it will empower those who read it.

Just as the elements of inner discontent merge into each other, so inner and outer sources of discontent overlap. It is to this second category that we now turn.

Outer Discontent

Outer discontent can take many forms, as illustrated in these words from a sales engineer.

> I was regional sales manager for (international manufacturing company) and my boss, it turned out, was essentially an alcoholic. It was a bad situation. He would get very rebellious, very tyrannical when he drank. He was impossible to live with.

> One time when we were on a sales trip to El Paso he was drinking and got mad and put his fist through the wall of my hotel room. That shot was really meant for me, I concluded, and I knew something had to change.

> The general manager of the division was a college professor, no more a businessman than my cat. He sat back and puffed his pipe and said, "Isn't this a great product!" when

our price was too high by twice and we were being killed in the marketplace.

My boss, the alcoholic, was dismissed just about the time I was ready to call it quits. I was living in L.A. at the time and got a job as a rep for a small company, working for people more attuned to the market.

Which source of discontent was more powerful? Was it the alcoholic boss or the inept division manager? Or was it some combination of the two exacerbated by hidden causes of discontent not apparent in an interview several years later?

Outer discontent comes from our work environment. As used here, environment means the "aggregate of all external conditions and influences" affecting us at work. We usually notice the physical part of our environment first: "What are the surroundings like at this work place?" Next we notice the interpersonal: "What are the people like here? What are the bosses like?" This leads us to the organizational environment: "What kind of an organization is this? What is it about?" The organization belongs to a group made up of others like it, perhaps an industry. Of this larger environment we may also ask: "What is it about?"

When we walk into a place of work our senses are bombarded with an overload of data.

Our eyes absorb the beauty or drabness of what is before us. We see brightness or dullness. We see differing levels of activity, differing numbers of people at work, differing layouts of the places where work is done. Our eyes pick up smiles or scowls. We see people dressed formally or casually. We see neatness or we see disarray. *All* of this is important and all can be a source of satisfaction... or a source of discontent.

Our ears give us a wealth of data, too. The decibel level in a woolen mill varies greatly from that in an architect's office. We may hear people yelling or we may hear more modulated tones. We may hear tension, fear, or anger in the voices of a workplace or we may hear laughter, affection, and concern. Again, our ears give us messages which can make us happy . . . or discontent.

Touching, smelling, and even tasting are also important. Do we feel dirt and grime when our fingers alight on desk tops or tool boxes? Do we encounter pleasant smells (for some, a bakery is heaven), or do we find that the smell of a place takes a few minutes getting used to? Do we like what our palate tells us about a place of work? Does it leave a good taste in our mouth?

Our physical environment can make all the difference. We need tools, whether typewriters or lathes, that are functional and modern enough so we can do our work without having to fight against devices designed to help us. We need at least the hope of improving our tools if necessary. We need proper light so our eyes can work without undue strain. We need sufficient ventilation so our lungs aren't filled with fumes and our heads aching at the end of the day.

If we work around hazardous substances we need adequate protection. The father of a friend has less than six months to live because of lung cancer traced to his working with asbestos in a shipyard during World War II. He did not have sufficient protection. Karen Silkwood was deeply concerned about the effects of radioactive material on herself and her co-workers in the lab where she worked; Silkwood has become a martyr for the cause of nuclear safety. Even cigarette smoke at the workplace is, for some, a health concern and a cause for discontent.

Physical risk at work can be a source of joy or a source of discontent. The steeplejack or the fireman may choose risky work because it is stimulating, rarely boring. All of us need some risk in our lives to keep us from vegetating. Yet a coalminer in Kentucky with five children and a mate to support may be deeply unhappy with the workplace risks produced by insufficient mine maintenance and inadequate ventilation. With no perceived employment options, this coalminer goes to work each day fearful and resentful and discontent.

Our place of work provides a broader perspective on our physical environment. Do we work in the city? in the suburbs? in the country? Working in the hustle and bustle of the metropolis is highly stimulating for some. For others, all those people and the hassles of commuting are just an aggravation. Some like the more casual environment often found at workplaces in the suburbs, with the chance to work close to home. For some this means a non-traditional commute, perhaps on foot or by bicycle, and this can be an important work benefit. And there are jobs out in the country, away from the noise of even the suburbs. Each of these choices can produce satisfaction . . . or discontent.

Related to the physical location of the place we work is its size. Some prefer to work with hundreds or thousands of others, enjoying the diversity and anonymity this environment offers. Others prefer a more compact environment, with just a few people, where closer relationships can form and each person gets the feeling of being special. Others prefer to work alone, or mostly alone. Whichever of these environments is right for us at this point in our lives, we face growing discontent if we make the wrong choice.

Our physical environment is different if we are employed by others or work for ourselves. While most of us work for others, there are thousands of ways we can work for ourselves, including starting our own business. Mohandas K. Gandhi was an advocate of cottage industry. For Gandhi, a hand loom in every home was preferable to hundreds of machinery driven looms in a huge factory; in his mind the advantages of worker-owned production tools and an integrated family life outweighed the advantages of specialized labor and high technology.

Also important is the question of what part of the world to work in. Since World War II, fewer Americans work in the same city where their parents worked, and we continue to be a mobile society. Women interested in marriage are advised by those in the know to try Chicago or Anchorage and to avoid San Francisco and Washington, D.C. Young men seeking adventure may choose to work in South America or Africa. The place is not important nor are the reasons for wanting to live there. What is important is that we notice our preferences about locale and become sensitive to the discontent that may arise from working in a part of the world that is not right for us.

Intertwined with the physical environment are interpersonal dimensions.

People-Related Discontent

The sales engineer who talked at the beginning of the last section about an alcoholic boss was facing an interpersonal problem. Almost all work involves people in some form, at some point. And where there are people, there are bound to be problems. The question we face in our worklife is whether the interpersonal dynamics are good, satisfactory, and tolerable, or do they cause sufficient discontent that change is required?

"The effectiveness of your life is determined by the effectiveness of your communication," Earl Nightingale said. The words you are reading now are a limited form of communication. The words we speak, facial expressions, body posture, clothing—all these communicate. Communication goes on all around us all the time in wild diversity. The satisfaction we get from our work, or the lack of it, is highly dependent on how well we communicate—how skillful we are at sending out messages and at interpreting those we receive.

The operative part of the word *communicate* comes from the Latin *communis*, which means "common." Thus, to communicate is to make common, to have knowledge and information available to those few or many involved in the process. Notice that this definition does not say that communication needs to be done with words, spoken or written. All that must happen is that knowledge must be "made common" among two or more persons.

Destructive communication usually springs from fear in the communicator. Someone who is living by a philosophy of poverty, with the overriding idea that there will never be enough, is usually a frustrating communicator. This is the person who withholds key inside information from a new employee so that the newcomer can "learn from experience, like I did." This is someone who refuses to loan the crucial tool to a co-worker. This philosophy of poverty, the fear that there is not enough for all of us, leads to inappropriate feelings of competitiveness and incomplete and unsatisfying communication.

Productive communication, on the other hand, often arises from a feeling of confidence in the communicator, from a philosophy of sufficiency. Confidence produces in the communicator the attitude that there is plenty of what is important in life and giving to another does not diminish that. A teacher of mine, an articulate professional, tells of how essential it was for him to find someone who would communicate with him honestly the first day he arrived at a federal penitentiary to serve six months. My friend is certain that if it had not been for the communicative inmate who taught him the rules of prison life, he would have left prison in a pine box.

Communication that springs from confidence leads to cooperation, whether in a prison setting or in a business office. This kind of communication often means that more gets done and those doing it feel better afterwards. Social scientists conduct experiments to see which conditions lead to competitive behavior. The reality of the world, it seems to me, is that there are elements of both competition *and* cooperation in any interaction involving two or more people. We err, in my experience, on the side of competitiveness, and this can lead to discontent.

The more I see relationships at work, the more I believe that *affirmation* builds relationship. If we want relationships that are durable and free flowing we need to affirm others, to communicate to them what we like about their work and what we appreciate about their work. In the play *My Fair Lady*, based on the Pygmalion myth, Professor Higgins is successful in transforming Eliza Doolittle at least in part because he *expects* that she is capable of change. Whatever else you may think about Higgins, he believes that Eliza *can* change, and makes this confidence known by affirming her progress; the rest is dramatic history.

In many work situations affirmation is hard because there is an underlying assumption that praise or thanks must be followed by some tangible reward. Money talks, it's said in business. Yet the communicator who is willing to risk breaking this norm by going beyond the old assumption has a rich opportunity for building relationships. Good communication, and particularly affirmation, builds relationships. Work without affirmation, to use the words of Camus at the head of this chapter, can be "stifling" and "soulless."

The third essential building block for fulfilling work is trust. Effective communication leads to durable relationships that lead to trust, the condition of trusting and being trusted. Trust in this sense means "reliance on another's integrity" and there must be enough of it for work to be satisfactory.

Although consistency—an important value among business managers—is one way to build trust, flexibility can also be important. The story is told of Gandhi's canceling on three days' notice a rally planned for thousands during his

48

campaign for Indian independence. As he explained to his incredulous associates, "I care more about truth than consistency." For Gandhi it was better to change his mind if the truth (as he saw it) changed so that the rally was no longer appropriate. What bridges this approach to trust with that of business managers is that both come from integrity, a kind of honesty that will not be denied.

Communication, relationship, trust. These are the building blocks for satisfaction at work.

Communication, relationship, and trust are threatened when we sense that we are not being treated fairly. We need to understand the basis for task assignments, for the allocation of the benefits of the job, for evaluation, and for compensation—money! Studies in the workplace indicate that dissatisfaction about money is *the* major source of discontent at work. And discontent feels the worst when we feel that we are not being treated fairly; we sense that others in the organization are getting a better deal than we are. Government figures indicate that women in this country earn fifty-nine cents for every dollar earned by men. Is it any wonder that many women are angry about unequal treatment?

Money discontent goes beyond interpersonal issues. We may be upset if the person next to us makes more than we do for the same work, but we will be equally unhappy if the dollars we earn are insufficient to meet our basic expenses. Money, which represents power and prestige and so much more than just exchange value, is a veritable wellspring of discontent.

Bosses

You may have noticed that no distinction has been made so far between relating to co-workers and to bosses. Bosses are different.

Power issues, discussed earlier, emerge in full bloom when bosses are involved. Bosses, after all, have power over our work assignments, our status and benefits, our compensation, and, ultimately, whether or not we may continue to work for the organization. A *lot* of power!

One way to understand relationships with bosses is to consider the fit between the people involved. If the boss wants to tell subordinates precisely what to do when, and one of the subordinates is a person who works best independently, there is a poor fit and trouble ahead. Conversely, if a worker is new and needs specific guidance and the boss is more comfortable with a hands-off approach, there is again a poor fit and another kind of trouble ahead.

For both bosses and subordinates, the path out of this dilemma is flexibility, the capacity to act differently where different action is required. The challenge each of us faces, however, is the always-shifting limit to our flexibility, and the key to this seems to be attitude. R. Buckminster Fuller, vigorous and active until his death at age eighty-five, reported that after going bankrupt at age twenty-six he decided that he was "going to work for everybody, everyone on the planet." This change in attitude changed his life, and led to contributions that have in fact benefited millions.

Flexibility and attitude determine how change happens. Our choices are to change ourselves or to try to change our boss; to change ourselves or to change our environment. Power comes from the ability to change ourselves, and the map laid out in this book is designed to help us do that. Through direct communication we may change our boss and change our environment (note that we do *not* have to leave the organization to change our work environment). But the change over which we have the most direct control is change within ourselves.

Discontent with a boss usually means that both of us are unhappy, perhaps in different degrees, usually in different ways. What happens? When nothing we do works, we may continue to live with our discontent. Like the British, we may muddle through. Or we can take the initiative and leave. Or our boss may take the initiative and fire us. Whatever the outcome, it represents a breakdown in communication, relationship, and trust, and the resulting discontent is best dealt with rather than left to smolder.

Organizations and Industries

Beyond physical and interpersonal sources of discontent, there may be organizational causes. Sometimes the organization we are working for is not right for us, and the discontent finally requires us to take notice and act. This kind of discontent may derive from the organization's mission, from its activities, or from its style.

The mission of an organization makes a big difference. A businessperson may see profit maximization as the transcendant organizational purpose, but a religious organization might have saving the world as its goal. The reason an organization exists can have a profound impact on how we feel about working there: the difference between the purposes of the American Red Cross and a small arms manufacturer is crucial for some.

The stated mission of an organization may differ from the actual mission or be at odds with some of the activities of an organization. The University of California, presumably an organization with an educational mission, has engaged in nuclear weapons research at its Lawrence Livermore Laboratories. Gregory Bateson, a University of California Regent at the time, questioned the incongruity of this, writing: "I believe that a university should have no connection with such folly, such evil (as nuclear weaponry). It's like a church or a hospital. The munitions of war should never be stored in such places or shipped in hospital ships. . . ."

Closely related to the mission of an organization are its

activities. The nature of the work, the diversity of tasks performed and the work pace can differ significantly between organizations. The "skinny white kid" who told of his baseball experience with his father at the start of this chapter has spent his entire business career with a major retailer. When he started, he told me, he was working twenty hours a day through one Christmas season and it got so bad that the company rented him an apartment across the street from the store so that he wouldn't have to take the subway uptown to where he normally lived. The hectic pace of retailing is not for all of us.

Small organizations usually offer a wide range of activities; large organizations are more likely to specialize. Some organizations deal primarily with people, others deal mainly with data, and still others work mostly with tangible objects. Some organizations work at a fast pace, others allow workers to set their own pace. If the nature, diversity, and pace of work in an organization do not fit for us, we are liable to be discontent.

A final organizational issue that can have a lot to do with satisfaction is organizational style. The style of an organization comes from its history, from its industry, from its customers or clients, and from the members of the organization, particularly its leaders. As with people, organizational style derives from underlying assumptions, from basic attitudes and beliefs. If the leaders of an organization see the members of that organization as unmotivated, uncreative, helpless and inferior, then the resulting style of the organization is likely to be authoritarian and oppressive—especially for those who do not fit those assumptions! If the leaders of an organization see the members as motivated, creative, autonomous and special, then the resulting style of the organization is likely to be democratic and supportive. For each organization a different style is appropriate. As members of organizations we need to determine if we can fit with the style of that organization, or whether we face rising discontent.

In recent years Americans have become increasingly aware of the management style found in Japanese businesses. These organizations usually provide lifetime employment, continual training, exposure to many parts of the business, and opportunities for all to participate in consensus-style decision making. American firms like Hewlett-Packard and Procter & Gamble have developed some of these same characteristics over the years with outstanding results. These organizations are right for their members. The question we face is what organization is right for us?

Beyond the question of organizations we face industry-wide sources of discontent. Such issues are very real for the person whose identity is "automobile worker" and whose paycheck no longer arrives because General Motors has closed the local plant. The worker who is uncomfortable working for a wine distributor may be equally uncomfortable working anywhere in the liquor industry. As new industries emerge, meeting new needs with new technology, we have expanded opportunities to find meaningful work . . . and the satisfaction we seek.

Where does discontent come from? It may be from our physical environment, from our interpersonal relationships, from the organizational environment, or even from the industry where we apply our talents. Wherever discontent comes from, our challenge is to recognize it and utilize it.

Discontent as Fuel

"I know it when I hear it but I can't tell you what it is," Louie Armstrong is supposed to have replied when asked to define good jazz. In the same way, we know discontent when we feel it. And though it is not essential to define this discontent, it is important to understand it well enough to do something about it, to turn it into motivation to get on with our lives.

"To love and to work ["*Lieben und arbeiten*"]," Freud answered, when asked what he thought a normal person should be able to do well. As living organisms we need to accomplish, to achieve—we need to work. Most of us work for money some forty hours a week, and that is the kind of work with which this book is most concerned. Some of the most important work in the world, however, is not done for money. Just ask Sister Teresa of Calcutta.

With unemployment in the ten percent range in much of the western world, many persons who want to work, and need to work, are not doing so. For these people the inborn need to be productive is compounded by the financial crunch of a truncated income. For those who are working there is often discontent, too. Do you doubt this? Talk with your friends. Read the newspapers. Look at the faces leaving the factory.

Discontent is like fuel. If we compare the human journey to a trip in an automobile, then there are benefits to having high power fuel and lots of it. The intensity of our discontent, like high-octane fuel, determines the extent of our journey—how far and how fast we move.

So if you feel some discontent, read on. Use that motivation, that special fuel, to move into the next chapter and discover ways to start preparing for your journey.

4

EXPLORATION:
OUR INNER WORLD

Nothing is hid that shall not be
Made manifest, nor anything secret
That shall not be known
And come to light.

LUKE 8:17

It is not only the most difficult
thing to know oneself, but the
most inconvenient one, too.

JOSH BILLINGS

Carl Jung taught that understanding our inner world is the first step toward gaining control of our lives. The pages that follow offer abundant opportunities for discovery in our inner worlds, and a chance to gain better control, particularly of our work lives.

In the career map unfolding in this book, exploration follows discontent. Well-grounded exploration begins by looking inward.

Looking inward expands our awareness of the forces which drive us, and those which hold us back. Our inner world holds the answers to our motivations and our inhibitions, our enthusiasms and our fears. From the energies in this inner world spring our likes and our dislikes, our sense of what interests us and what bores us. The locus of our soul and our spiritual center, our inner world is the wellspring for our response to life.

"Know thyself," Socrates said. This is the point where we take control of the journey. No assignment can be more important. For, in the words of Luke at the head of this chapter, ultimately "Nothing is hid."

To know ourselves we first look backward.

Looking Backward

It is no mystery why prospective employers look at past performance more closely than anything else in making a hiring decision. What we have done in the past is still the best indicator of what we will do in the future. Our achievements in school, in previous jobs, in the military all provide tangible evidence of what we might achieve in the future (the leopard does not change his spots). Valuable clues come from our history in the areas of relationships, perseverence, productivity, promptness, even health. So it is appropriate that we also examine our past, but in more depth than a personnel manager would.

We start by recreating our past. The best way for you to do this as part of your inner exploration is to write out your personal work life history. To do this, first write down along the left hand side of a sheet of paper *all* the jobs you have had and the dates (6/77-9/77 or 1974-76, etc.). Start with your first job, whether paid or not, whether as a baby-sitter or as a paper boy. Use as many sheets as you need. Now go back over your list and in the second column put all the things you liked about that job, and in the third column put all the things you did not like. Take your time; be thorough. In the fourth and final column put what you feel to be your most important accomplishment in that job. When you have completed this work you will have created a treasure chest from which enormous value can spring.

This exercise is done near the beginning of most career change workshops I lead, and it works. The first benefit of the worklife history is that it illustrates in black and white that we *do* have a lot of valuable experience. We have already accomplished a lot. This exercise also highlights our interests (roughly, our likes and dislikes) and starts us thinking about our skills (usually illustrated by our accomplishments). This history contains reflections of our inner world that might not otherwise appear.

The first ten of the Tools for Exploration found in Appendix A are a means for you to gain additional insights, and the Twenty-Question Career Quiz found in Appendix B will give you a better sense of where you are on the career-cycle. I suggest that you look at these now and decide which, if any, you want to do next and which you want to take time for later.

Have you ever kept a journal? This can be a rich resource for introspection into your work life. There are several good books on journal keeping, the best by Ira Progoff. If you start now you will have a concrete means for reviewing your impressions and progress two months from now.

Moving further toward the intuitive, further into the right hemisphere of the brain, art can be a valuable tool for exploring our inner world. Try this assignment. On a sheet of newsprint use crayons, pastels, felt tip markers, whatever, to draw a picture of your life as you would like it to be. Draw it as an island and include there all the people and things and activities you want in your work life. Beside each major element on your island list which of your interests are represented there. Beside that make a list of which of your skills are represented.

If you want to move even further into the intuitive, draw with your left hand (unless you are left-handed, in which case you would use your right, right?).

When you have completed the two lists, take a dark color and draw fences to represent the barriers you have created to keep you from having your life as you would like it to be. These barriers should then be labeled. They might be fear of success, unwillingness to commit, resistance to change, poor self image, lack of money, or frustration with this exercise. You decide. But be honest and build and label the barriers as accurately as you can.

The next step is to find a friend and tell this person what your picture means to you. Better yet, find a friend who will do his or her own picture, and then tell each other what you have discovered. Islands give the illusion of separateness, surrounded on all sides by water, but remember that at a deeper level all islands are connected, just as all people, are connected at some level. Working with someone else on this exercise helps you to see this.

Recognizing barriers is a giant step toward breaking them down and is critical to our success in finding the right work, as we shall see.

There are ways to go further with this art exercise, and with barriers in particular. One approach is illustrated by the following abbreviated dialog from a recent workshop. The first speaker, a thirty-two-year-old called Joel here, is describing a barrier to the group.

Joel: Probably my biggest barrier is that I don't think I'm good enough to get the things I want in life.

John: Would you like to work on that issue?

Joel: Yes.

John: Scan back in your life, looking for a point when this feeling of not being good enough was particularly strong. And when you are there, when the picture is clear, tell us about it.

Joel: I remember when I was seventeen I borrowed my father's new car and it needed oil. After putting in a quart of oil, I forgot to put the cap back on the crankcase and drove home that way.

The next morning I was going to use the car again and it wouldn't start. So I thought I'd roll start it and was pushing the car out of the garage. But I had left the car door open and it swung into the side of the garage and the car jerked to a stop with this horrible crunch. God!

I felt really stupid. I felt terrible. And I knew my dad would be *really* pissed.

John: Take yourself back to that time, at age seventeen. Be that seventeen-year-old and tell us how you feel.

Joel: (at age seventeen) I really screwed up. I was really dumb. I feel dumb, hopeless.

John: Now shift places and be your father and create a dialog between father and seventeen-year-old Joel.

Joel: (as father) You're always fucking up! What's wrong with you? Can't you do anything right? Can't I trust you with *anything*?

Joel: (at age seventeen) I did the best I could. I *tried* to take good care of the car.

Joel: (as father) Tried? You tried? I think you are a total fuck-up. I can't trust you with anything.

John: See if he understands.

Joel: (at age seventeen) Can't you see that I was trying to do my best? That I'm usually reliable, that you can count on me, like in school?

Joel: (as father) Yeah, you do have some good points (laughter). You do some stuff well.

John: See if he forgives seventeen-year-old Joel.

Joel: (as father) Yeah, I understand. I can forgive you, Joel. I forgive you, Joel (tears).

Joel: Yeah. I see. Whew!

In this session Joel went into his barrier to try to reconcile the force which was blocking him. He relived the fear of the seventeen-year-old and the anger of the father as two sides of the thirty-two-year-old adult. In reliving this experience Joel brought the two sides closer together, moved toward integrating two parts of his personality, and in the process removed some of the energy from behind his "not good enough" block.

A note of caution. The psychological work Joel did took place in a safe and secure environment, with a high trust level and high level of support from the group leader, group members, and workshop staff. This cannot happen in most places and is not for everyone.

A final example of such work illustrates an approach to dealing with another kind of block. In this dialog, a thirty-six-year-old physician, called Mary here, deals with a barrier to her transition to professional photographer.

Mary: One of my barriers is guilt. I feel it's wrong to give up medicine, after all my training. And yet I know photography is right for me. It's really got me confused.

John: Would you like to work on that?

Mary: Yes. Please.

John: Could you talk some more about the feelings of guilt?

Mary: All my life I've been brought up to take care of others, my younger brothers, and now my patients . . . and my husband. It's like this voice is saying, "Mary, you're no good unless you're helping someone." It's like my mother is saying———

John: Be your mother. Put yourself in your mother's place and talk to Mary.

Mary: (as mother) Mary . . . Mary, you know that good girls help other people. You know it's important to think of them first, think of their needs first, before your own.

John: What does Mary say back? Create a dialog.

Mary: (as child—with feeling) Yes, I know all that. You've told me that *lots* of times before. But I have a life too, and I have a right to live.

Mary: (as mother) Yes, dear, but you shouldn't be so selfish. You should think of others less fortunate.

Mary: (as child) Baloney! I've done that. I've been doing that for too long. For *too long!* (tears).

Mary: (as mother) Yeah, well. Maybe it is OK for you to give some time for yourself. You *are* a very creative person, you know.

Mary: Yeah. I'd like that. That seems right.

John: What do you learn from these two parts?

Mary: Well, you know, the part of me that wants to help is OK. I'm damn good at it. And maybe the little girl part, the carefree, creative part that loves to take photographs fits in there, too. That part of me is all right, too. That part helps people, too, with the art.

In this session, Mary looked at the guilt that was blocking her from further exploration. In a confrontation between the mother in her and the child in her, Mary moved toward seeing that both sides have value. Mary moved toward completing the gestalt, the circle of her wholeness. Both parts, she sees, have something to offer. And both need to be recognized and appreciated as she continues to explore career development options.

Notice that in Mary's work an important element is introduced briefly when she mentions her husband. In the career change process, the role of our partner or others who are significant in our lives is inextricably bound up with the decisions we make. It is an area of mutual responsibility, that will re-emerge at several points in coming pages.

Like many of the tools described here, intense psychological work like that done by Joel and Mary is an approach which is appropriate for *some* people in *some* situations. It is not for everyone. It is not essential or even desirable for many who feel discontent. For the rest, however, psychological exploration done with skillful and sensitive guidance *can* be a powerful means for refocusing work-related energy.

In looking backward we start with a written exercise—our work life history—and move from there to other learning techniques, including journal keeping, drawing the life we want and the barriers we have created, and even working intensely with those barriers.

Do you notice how time past intermingles with time present and even time future, just as the physical, mental, emotional, and intuitive dimensions intermingled in Chapter Three? It is convenient to arrange time in three dimensions and it is also important to see how time is of a single fabric.

Or as T. S. Eliot wrote in "Burnt Norton":

Time present and time past
Are both perhaps present in time future,
And time future contained in time past.

Looking at Now

In Lewis Carroll's *Alice's Adventures in Wonderland*, the caterpillar asks, "Who are you?"

"I hardly know, Sir, just at present," Alice replied rather shyly, "at least I know who I *was* when I got up this morning, but I think I must have changed several times since then."

We all change continuously and there's no time like the present. Philosophers from various traditions tell us of the value of living in the moment; and this advice applies to our inner exploration. What we are doing, thinking, feeling right now provides us with a wealth of information about choices in work.

How are you applying your productive energies right now? We can learn a great deal from our present or most recent job, from the volunteer work we are doing, from the courses we are taking in school as well as our extracurricular activities there, from our avocations and hobbies, even from our entertainments.

Start with a job, current or recent. What interests you in this job? What bores you? What do you do well? And, being honest, what don't you do so well? What have been your most rewarding accomplishments? What else? Take your time and get it all down.

What do you like about this job? What do you enjoy most? What gives you pleasure? Forget the Puritan work ethic that says that if it is fun it must be bad. Work is a source of joy. Notice where your joy comes from.

Joyce, a twenty-two-year-old recent college graduate, wants to break out of the accounting rut she has worked in the last two years. Listen to what she discovered about her present job, a part-time bookkeeping position:

> In looking at what gave me the most pleasure, I realized that it was unraveling the mess in the equipment leasing department. The records were all over the place. No one could find a lease agreement when they needed it.

> I sorted through tons of files, threw out what wasn't needed, and organized what was. I got the secretaries to help. I got the department manager to set up categories for the new files and with her help I trained the secretaries and the salesmen to use the new system. It works great. No problems. And I feel really proud of my contribution.

Within her "bookkeeping" job Joyce found that she enjoys problem solving, organizing data, training others, and persuading others—to identify just a few of the skills that she used in this project. Joyce does not have to define herself narrowly as an accountant, but can expand her vision of employment by seeing herself as a manager or trouble-shooter or

65

consultant or any one of a number of other job targets that her skills and interests make appropriate for her. By seeing her present job with new eyes, Joyce gains new understanding of her options.

Our interests, enthusiasms, and impulses in our present lives all provide clues for our future direction. All are relevant. All are worth writing down and reviewing.

Part of what all this reflects is our values. Values are important because they determine how we live. Values come from our parents, siblings, teachers, bosses, peers, mentors, heros, political leaders—from whomever and whatever we are exposed to. Parents, in particular, are important, as with this top executive I interviewed recently:

> If I am totally honest, I have to say that the person who had the most influence on me was my mother. She was way ahead of her time. She smoked when women didn't smoke. She was devout and totally dedicated to people. We grew up in an orange grove in Southern California and her family would go without before she would let the workers go hungry.
>
> She sat us three boys down and told us about sex. That made us smug as hell in school. She was daring, a real educator.

These words about his formative years tell us much about this man and his values today. He is candid, daring, and devotes a big part of his work energy to making life better for others.

How can we better understand our own values? Take a few minutes and read the following story, which was supposedly first heard on a TV show a few years ago:

> Once upon a time there was a woman named Abigail who was in love with a man named Gregory. Gregory lived on

the shore of a river and Abigail lived on the other shore. The river which separated the two lovers was teeming with man-eating alligators.

Abigail wanted to cross the river to be with Gregory. Unfortunately, the bridge had been washed out. So she went to ask Sinbad, a river boat captain, to take her across. Sinbad said that he would be glad to if she would consent to go to bed with him preceding the voyage. She promptly refused and went to a friend named Ivan to explain her plight. Ivan did not want to be involved at all in the situation.

Abigail felt that her only alternative was to accept Sinbad's terms. Sinbad fulfilled his promise to Abigail and delivered her into the arms of Gregory.

When Abigail told Gregory about her amorous escapade in order to cross the river, Gregory cast her aside with disdain. Heartsick and dejected, Abigail turned to Slug with her tale of woe. Slug, moved by Abigail's story, sought out Gregory and beat him brutally. Abigail was overjoyed at the sight of Gregory getting his due. As the sun sets on the horizon, we hear Abigail laughing at Gregory.

Now reread the story, paying close attention to how you feel about each of the five characters. When you are through with this second reading take a sheet of paper and rank the five characters, with the person you find *most* offensive ranking first, and the person you find *least* offensive ranking fifth. When you have done this, write your reasons for each choice in a few short phrases. Finally, beside each name write the values you see acted out by the characters (loyalty, flexibility, honesty, helpfulness, and the like).

Do you see how the values tend to come in opposites, containing both positives and negatives? Abigail is flexible, resourceful, and loving, yet she is also fickle, unscrupulous, and vengeful. Sinbad is direct and reliable, yet is also exploitative and unsympathetic. Our own value systems contain such paired opposites, and both the positive and negative values are important in choices about work.

Considering what you have learned about your own values, how good is your fit at work? If you value involvement (finding Ivan offensive) and the organization where you work values only profit making, some shift may be in order. If you value achievement and the organization where you work focusses mainly on human interactions like teaching, you might reassess your role there.

Although "Alligator River" teaches us about our values in the workplace, it also tells us something about our values in relationships. The romantic dilemmas of Abigail and Gregory are relevant because all of us have faced those same issues in one guise or another.

Part of our inner exploration involves asking about the attitudes and values of our partners and others in our lives who are affected by how we work. Money is a hot issue. There are a multitude of issues around money, but essentially they boil down to who is responsible for providing how much. Closely related to money is the issue of time, and here it is not only how much time but how it is spent, and when, and with whom. Will work be done at home and if so how does that fit with others who may live there? What about travel? How much time away from home is right in your life? How about children? If children are involved, who is responsible for the various kinds of adult involvement children require? And how do the children feel about it?

A former grade school teacher told me the following story:

> I was about to lose my teaching job due to declining enrollment and the only other jobs I was interested in paid considerably less than the $20,000 a year I was making. I felt stuck.
>
> Then I got to thinking. My husband has an excellent income as a surgeon and the extra dollars I earned don't

affect our lives much. What's important, and my husband agrees, is that I find fulfilling work. Now I feel like I have a lot more options.

This woman examined her values and found that money was not nearly as important to her as satisfying work. As a result of her realization, everyone benefits. Tools #13 and #14 in Appendix A offer further insight on attitudes toward money.

In working to mesh our values with those of others in our life, it is helpful to remember that work can have value for those around us in a myriad of ways. The weaver who works at home so his children can see his work progressing offers special benefits. The manager who can include her children in an office lunch or business trip provides a unique teaching. The teacher who can relate to the students in his own house provides a rich supplement to their classroom experience. And there are a number of other ways partners can benefit from our work—ranging from health care benefits to new social involvement to the stimulations of hearing new ideas and sharing in new enthusiasms at the dinner table.

What our examination of our interests, accomplishments, pleasures, skills, attitudes, and values all points to is the answer to the question: Who am I? A tool for further inner exploration that can be helpful at this point is to take ten sheets of paper and at the top of each write: "Who am I?" After writing a different answer on each sheet make three lists, with the values, interests, and skills that support the identity at the top of that sheet. Then spread the ten sheets on the floor and pick the three most important and the three least important. See what job indications come from the top three; watch how "Who am I?" leads to "What should I be doing with this life of mine?"

This ten-sheet exercise is adopted from Richard Bolles, who has also created the best single tool for helping us identify our skills. Called "The Quick Job-Hunting Map" (and available separately and at the back of *What Color is*

Your Parachute?), these few pages provide an excellent listing of skills and provide a way for us to find which ones belong to us. In classes and workshops where I have used this tool, we found it to be challenging work and well worth every minute invested.

Whether you complete the "Quick Job-Hunting Map" or not, there is an important piece of work I suggest for wrapping up this section. Find a friend, perhaps the one you worked with on the art exercise earlier in this chapter, and tell your friend what skills you want to employ in your work life. Take your time. Brag a little, brag a lot. If you know what kinds of things you want to achieve with your skills, so much the better. Tell your friend about that, too. When you are finished, ask for feedback from your friend: What did your friend hear? How did it sound? What could be added? At that point, make notes—this is *valuable*—and repeat the process.

Most of us have been taught things like "Children should be seen and not heard" and "Nice girls don't brag." For this journey those old voices are no longer relevant. It is crucial to know ourselves, and to let others know us, too.

Looking Forward

The future is important because that is where we will spend the rest of our lives. Our hopes and dreams for the future can tell us much about our inner world.

In this section we will explore our inclinations toward prescience. We will give shape to our fantasies and see what can be learned from them. We are especially aware here of entering into the realm of risk, a part of the journey where uncertain outcomes increase our danger and demand that we be fully attentive.

The most simple question is often the best place to

begin. And the best beginning is often to ask the question: What do you *think* you want to do, work-wise? Consider this question for a moment and jot down whatever comes to mind. Keep going, even if you already have three or four ideas. In most initial career counseling sessions I ask this question at some point, and I find that most clients have some idea of what they want to do. And I find that this wished-for career usually makes sense in terms of the interests and values and skills of the people describing their dreams.

To move further in this direction, consider another question: If someone burst in the door right this minute and said, "Guess what? You have just been given all the money you'll ever need, tax-free," what would you *then* want to do with the work part of your life? Let your mind range freely and write down the ideas which emerge.

Do you doubt the value of such fantasies? Notice these words from Albert Einstein:

> When I examined myself and my methods of thought, I came to the conclusion that my gift of fantasy has meant more to me than my talent for absorbing positive knowledge.

If one of the greatest scientists of this century places such a value on fantasy, it is a tool worth our developing.

Moving one level deeper, we can work with fantasy that taps into our subconscious mind, that part that is not normally available on a day to day basis. To do this, find a quiet place where you will not be disturbed for a few minutes, close your eyes, quieting down inside, and then let yourself drift ahead five years in time. Start at the beginning of your day, in your mind's eye, getting up and eating breakfast. Notice where you go to work, who is there, what you do. Take plenty of time to look around. At the end of your work day, come home, again observing your surroundings, have the evening meal, and when you are ready, climb back into bed. Now come back into time present and open your eyes.

You have just used active imagination, a mild form of self-hypnosis, to look at pieces of your hopes and dreams that your conscious mind might not let you see.

Most of my experience in working with this "day in the future" has involved guided imagery with individual clients or with groups. In groups, the individuals later work in pairs and describe to each other the content of their "day." You might also find a friend to discuss this with, since the result can be quite powerful, providing important clues about work-life, relationships, even living spaces. Although some of us are more responsive to this kind of fantasy than others, almost all who work with it derive some value.

A more personal way of working with the subconscious is through dreams. "A dream not understood is like a letter unopened," says the Talmud, and dreams that involve our work life can provide particularly valuable insights. Dreams can help us understand discontent that stems from work, and the pre-cognitive dreams some have can offer clues about future directions in work. Researchers say that dreams are necessary for the restoration of emotional equilibrium. Dreams are equally essential for equilibrium at work.

You can write your dreams in a notebook, discuss them with a friend, analyze them with a counselor. The goal is to integrate your subconscious into your waking awareness and, in the process, increase your understanding of what you want in life and in work. The ways for doing this are both diverse and complex and I suggest that you read books on dream work, attend a dream workshop, or even meet with a Jungian therapist if you want to work with your dreams in depth.

How about looking even farther into the future?

Imagine that you are your own best friend, someone

who has known "you" well for a lifetime. "You" have just died, after a long, full life, and the local newspaper needs someone to write "your" obituary. So they ask you, as the best friend of the deceased, to write the life story of this fine person, now sadly missed. What were this person's accomplishments? What was this person known for? What quotations from family, friends, professional associates can you include about this person? What were the last ten years of this person's life like? The last twenty years? Fill in the important details from time present to the time (how many years are left?) when this well-loved person departs this earth.

When you have written this obituary—and don't spare any words—go back over it and look for patterns. Make a list of the interests which are reflected there. Make a similar list for skills and one for values. Finally, write down three action steps that you need to take in the next sixty days to start to achieve what the obituary says you will achieve.

If you have been doing the work suggested in this chapter you will by now have a better sense of where you want to go. If you want to do further work on your own, turn again to Appendix A and try several of the second ten of the twenty Tools for Exploration described there. Do you notice the pieces of the puzzle starting to come together? Are patterns starting to appear and make sense? In all likelihood you are getting some clues on the direction to move in.

If at this stage you still do not have any idea what you want to do next, you might try more reading and exercises. *What Color is Your Parachute?* is the best for this, I find, and *The Hidden Job Market for the '80s* by Jackson and Mayleas is also excellent. If this doesn't do it, the next step is to sign up for a career workshop at a local high school, junior college, or university extension. These are usually good, almost-always low cost courses that have the significant benefit of getting you together with people in the same boat you are in. If this fails, find a career counselor at a local clinic or college (where there is a small charge or none at all) or a career counselor in private practice.

Most of us go to career counselors when we think we are lost, when we are literally unsure about where we are in the world of work. The skillful counselor, having helped us to find ourselves, will help us to see options on where we might go from here. The counselor will also provide specific coaching, if we need it, on how to get there. More information on career counseling, if you want it, is presented in Appendix C at the end of the book.

I have read the books I recommend (and done the exercises in them and used them in classes and workshops) and I have attended career workshops of different kinds and I have had some valuable career counseling. Each of these paths can help, and I encourage you to explore them if you feel the need for more help.

You might decide to continue reading into the next chapter to see if you can discover there what you need. Before that, though, it is worth pausing to look at a little map of a piece of the territory we are traversing.

Mini-Map

A road map for the state of Colorado shows the towns of various sizes and the roads that lead to each. The Colorado road map also includes an insert with a larger scale map of the city of Denver which shows roads that are important to the traveler and that could not be read if they were on the same scale as the state map. This mini-map helps the driver find his way in Denver. In the last paragraphs of this chapter we will look at a mini-map that covers in detail the exploration portion of the larger careercycles map described in this book.

This mini-map derives from the scientific method.

Any time we drive an automobile or make a telephone call we benefit from the scientific method. The scientific method of problem solving is to develop an hypothesis, say, that a buggy can be driven by a gasoline engine. We then gather information, say, by building an engine and putting it in a buggy. The next step is to analyze the information, say, by getting the contraption to run and recording what happens. Finally, in the scientific method we draw conclusions, in the case of the horseless buggy that perhaps the hypothesis has validity and should be explored further by repeating the process. So much for Henry Ford.

In Figure 6, the scientific method is applied to career exploration. This map shows the steps above and illustrates the increasing involvement of other people as the process progresses.

What this map says, first of all, is that we go through a logical, fairly predictable sequence of steps as we approach change in our worklife. We develop an idea about what we want, we check it out and in the process of collecting infor-

FIGURE 6

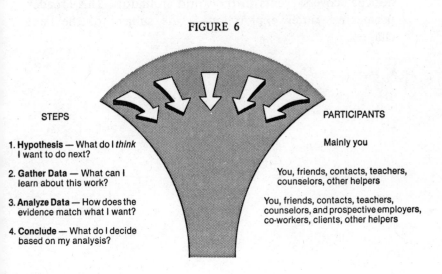

STEPS

1. **Hypothesis** — What do I *think* I want to do next?

2. **Gather Data** — What can I learn about this work?

3. **Analyze Data** — How does the evidence match what I want?

4. **Conclude** — What do I decide based on my analysis?

PARTICIPANTS

Mainly you

You, friends, contacts, teachers, counselors, other helpers

You, friends, contacts, teachers, counselors, and prospective employers, co-workers, clients, other helpers

mation we are continually analyzing: How does this fit for us? How should we modify our original hypothesis? How do we get more information? Finally, when we have enough data and have mulled it over enough to suit our particular penchant for thoroughness, we reach a conclusion. At about that time someone with the power to hire should be reaching the same conclusion, and we have the job offer we have been seeking.

In the beginning the process is mostly us, perhaps with a friend involved (who may be our partner or a family member). As we go out in the world we need to get others involved because we need more information. So, in addition to friends we use our contacts and use teachers, counselors, workshop leaders, librarians, therapists, whatever helpers we need. As we approach a conclusion, we move further into the world by including in the process, in addition to those already involved, people who have the power to employ our skills in solving their problems. The decision we are seeking is then made jointly, by consensus—which is what we want.

The major portion of this mini-map, as you may have noticed, covers events in the world around us. This broader perspective—outer exploration—is the subject of the next chapter.

5

EXPLORATION:
THE WORLD
AROUND US

Whatever you can do, or dream
you can, begin it.
Boldness has genius,
power, and magic in it.

GOETHE

If you can meet with triumph and disaster
And treat those two imposters just the same.

RUDYARD KIPLING

Exploration is hard ... and it is rewarding. Exploration sometimes pushes us to our limits ... and it brings out the best in us. In exploration we often face grave risks ... which make us feel more alive than ever before. In this chapter, the map for career development continues to unfold, with the focus on exploring the world around us.

The exploration of our inner world in the last chapter flows into the exploration of the world around us. The foundation we laid in examining our inner world is essential to success in looking at the outer world. Just because we start to focus our attention outward does not mean that the inner messages are ignored: new understandings of our interests, values, and skills continue to develop as we explore the world around us.

How does outer exploration begin? We notice things like this recent newspaper column titled "Firms Thriving in Recession," which observes that unlike firms in the steel, auto, cement, timber, and aluminum industries, some companies are prospering:

> For Grand Auto, Inc. for instance, the recession means record profits and sales.
>
> The Oakland-based auto supply chain, whose stock is listed on the American Stock Exchange, reported earlier this week the figures for its fiscal year ended January 31 (1982.) Grand Auto's sales were up twenty percent, net profit was up twenty-five percent to $2.69 a share versus $2.16 in the previous fiscal year.
>
> A good percentage of Grand Auto's sales—$119.9 million in the recent twelve months—were made to customers who normally would let an auto repair shop do minor work on their cars.

If you have mechanical skills and interests would this article spark any ideas? You bet! Here is a clue to opportunity for someone with the ability to refurbish cars, paint cars, install new equipment on cars, hook up stereos in cars or vans, or in general make an existing vehicle work better, go further, and look nicer ... at a reasonable cost. Or if you like retail sales, you might consider working for an auto parts supplier ... like Grand Auto.

Library Research

The fact that you are reading this sentence indicates that you know something about the value of the written word. Millions of these words, some quite helpful, are available in newspapers, magazines, government reports, corporate financial statements, tracts, manuals, pamphlets, and books of various kinds. Information can be found in these diverse forms in many places, but probably the one best place to look is the public library. There are also high school libraries, college libraries, government libraries (some Federal Reserve Bank branches, for instance, have excellent libraries), libraries maintained by organizations or corporations, and libraries owned by private individuals.

Here is how a single book made a crucial difference for one career changer, reported in her own words:

> As a re-entry woman I figured the only way I was going to get a job was with secretarial skills, so I took a course in office occupational skills at a local junior college. I realized pretty soon that I didn't want to do secretarial work full time.
>
> The woman who taught this secretarial class was very interested in helping us get jobs. She brought in this woman from the government unemployment department who mentioned a book, *How to get work when your husband's against it, your kids are too young, and there's nothing you can do anyway.*
>
> I was so impressed that I went to see this woman at her office, talk some more, and borrow her book. Among other things, the book had ways to convert skills, interests, and volunteer work into specific careers. One was editing.
>
> I had a flash of insight. Editing was it. I still remember the moment, in an afternoon in the fall of 1978. I'm working full time as an editor now, and I love it.

You may not find "the answer" in a single book, but if you have two or three job ideas from the last chapter, the library is the place to begin to check them out. Your friendly reference librarian can help you find industry directories if you want to learn more about a particular industry and the companies in it. If you are interested in marketing management, for instance, the *Redbook of Advertising* lists companies by area, with the amount of advertising dollars spent and the names of company officers. Many cities have directories of local employers that provide an excellent resource for identifying nearby companies in the fields which interest you. The options are almost endless. As an explorer, the challenge is to keep looking, keep asking questions, keep reading.

If you are still looking for ideas, you might spend some time with the *Dictionary of Occupational Titles*, published by the U.S. Government Printing Office in Washington, D.C. This three volume resource cross-references occupations by interests and aptitudes. It lists over 35,000 job titles and is an excellent reference book.

Like each of the points on this map of career development, the library is a place to which we return. The printed word provides important guidance at *many* points along the way.

Friends, Acquaintances, and Other Contacts

Sooner or later we need to talk to people who know something about the work we want to do. These may be friends we seek out, or acquaintances we see at parties or the supermarket, or strangers we sit next to on the bus. Once we have some idea of where we want to go, we have something important to talk about. We have an hypothesis to check out.

Listen to the words of one career changer:

> When I was thinking about going into college teaching full time, my wife heard from a friend at her college reunion about a conference of AIDS (the American Institute of Decision-making Sciences, an organization of university teaching professionals). It was in downtown Atlanta, so I went.
>
> It was a super experience. I found that I knew a lot about the topics discussed. And I was interested in them. The textbooks on display were fascinating, too.

I went by the placement room which had two full books of job openings. I learned about starting salaries and job requirements and who was hiring and where. I wrote down several local names for follow-up later.

The most important thing I got from that conference, though, was that I felt comfortable around all those college professors. I felt more at home with them than with the business managers I had been dealing with. This gave me a real strong sense that I was moving in the right direction, that teaching might be right for me.

There is lots and lots of value in attending a conference or convention or trade show or otherwise getting close to those doing the kind of work we think we want to do. We hear people talking about the work, we see them interacting with each other, and we often see them doing the work. Whether we do a little or a lot of this, we are initiating important contacts and advancing our research.

Networking is using friends and friends of friends to get what we want. The "old boy network" has been operated by mature white males for almost as long as business has been done in this country, and it continues intact because of its effectiveness. Each of us, however, regardless of our age and color and gender can build our own network by talking to friends and tapping into the network represented by their friends and contacts. How? We need to ask, to assert ourselves, to initiate. It is a rare friend indeed who will not help when asked. Try it and see.

In exploring career options, no one can do it for us. We need to tap into our network of friends and contacts ourselves. Like the prospective college teacher, we need to go to the conference in person; we cannot send a surrogate. No one can do our exploring for us. Not long ago a man I know wanted to leave the Forest Service; he paid a national company several thousand dollars to find him a new career, write his resume, and deliver him a job offer. It's very tempting to try to find someone else to take the journey for us, to do the hard work, but like many short cuts, it doesn't work. For my friend, this short cut was a debacle and though he never got his money back, he did find a new and satisfying career on his own—by doing his own exploring.

Workshops, Classes, and Degrees

"If you think education is expensive, try ignorance," says Derek Bok, president of Harvard University. All exploration is education in the broadest sense of the word, but structured educational programs have a special place in the exploration process. Workshops, seminars, extension classes, and degree-awarding programs all have potential value for the explorer.

The career changer quoted earlier in this chapter used an office skills class as a springboard into an editing job. She is presently enhancing her job and strengthening her position with her company by working on a certificate program in editing through a nearby university extension. For her, formal education is one way to continue exploring.

Workshops, seminars, and courses are a fine way to continue learning, but beware of pursuing a degree as a way to avoid starting now with a career. When someone says to me, "I can't get a job there without an MBA," I remind them that what employers want, even those who specify a degree for a particular job, is a person with the *skills* to solve their problems.

Workplace Research

The research you do should not be limited to talking with friends or attending workshops. These are valuable early sources of information but even more crucial to your investigation are those doing the kind of work you want to do in the actual place where that work is done.

To get this information from the workplace you need to set up meetings with the appropriate people. The word "meeting" is used here consciously. "Meeting" means to come together by mutual agreement, and implies a gathering of two or more equals for a particular purpose. The word "interview" is often used at this stage and it, by contrast, has come to refer to a coming together of two or more people who are not equals. *Interview* comes from the French word *entrevoir* meaning "to see imperfectly, have a glimpse of" or "visit each other." Presidents and movie stars and authors are interviewed. While interviewing is also an essential part of finding work, meetings are more appropriate at this point. Interviews come later.

There are a number of reasons why research meetings are preferable to employment interviews at this point in the cycle. The better you understand these reasons, the more successful your meetings will be. Look at the differences:

Employment interviews	*Research meetings*
Employer takes initiative.	You take initiative.
Employer usually has to say no because most job applicants are rejected.	Employer can say yes because people enjoy giving information.
Employer worried about making a mistake by hiring wrong person.	Employer not threatened by hiring decision, can be relaxed.
Employer is tense and so are you.	Employer is at ease and so are you.
Usually no one emerges a winner.	Almost always both emerge winners.

The reason research meetings work is that they allow you to collect the information you need to put your skills to work at the same time they allow employers a chance to publicize their organization *and* get a look at people they might want to hire. (Good people are the life blood of *any* organization.) Your goal as an explorer is to collect information, and you need the easiest way to get the type and amount of information required. Explorers so far have found that the research meeting is that way.

With whom should you meet? You pick the highest priority target area for your next job, and then find someone in an organization doing that work at about the level you are interested in. If you are considering public relations, for instance, there is a good chance you know someone in the field, perhaps because this person stimulated your interest in the first place. If this person is the prime prospect for the job you want, you would not start there until you had more facts and some experience with research meetings. You want a warm up at this point, not your number one target.

What if you do not know a single person in the area you are interested in? You try friends of friends first—networking. In the research you have done already you probably met people who know people who you could meet with. Failing that, you could ask a counselor or teacher for a name to get you started. And failing that, you can head back to the library and develop a list of prospects (which you want to do before long anyway) from which to pick the first person you meet with.

If you would like to see one way *not* to get to see people, read this classified advertisement that appeared recently in a weekly newspaper:

JOB WANTED

Brilliant Grad School Returnee
seeks interesting lucrative p/t
job w/flex hours. Wide exper.
555-1224 after 10am

An ill-defined goal is just one of this job seeker's problems.

If you would like to learn techniques which have successfully gained interviews for other explorers, read on.

Getting Appointments

Some people have an easier time getting appointments than others. Some are more glib. Some are more comfortable approaching people cold on the telephone. Some just have an easier time speaking with people they have not met before. No matter. If you take the time to understand the process involved and are willing to take a little coaching on the words to use, you can do as well as anyone, wherever you're starting from.

Working from the larger goal of collecting the data you need to be successful in your explorations, the immediate goal is to get the targeted person to see you, face to face. You do not want to be interviewed over the telephone because the value of an in the flesh meeting is many times greater—the sensory data you collect is vastly larger if you visit the workplace in person, and the information available to the person you meet with is also much greater. So your goal is a personal meeting, not a telephone discussion, and not a turn-down.

Even before starting, examine your attitude. Do you recognize that rejection is a part of life? Do you see that every successful human being faces many rejections in moving ahead? Can you accept that rejection is part of getting what you want?

Between drafts of this chapter I took time to counsel with a former minister who has been unemployed for three years, since being forced out of his position as head of a social service organization. "If only I could get that first interview," he told me, "I know I could get a job." When pressed he acknowledged, "I guess I fear rejection. I don't want a repeat of the experience I had in losing my last job." We *all* dislike rejection. It's no fun for anyone. But if we see it as part of a process leading to acceptance, our attitude changes. Just as brushing our teeth is essential to dental health, rejection is part of getting what we want.

Look at it this way. There are a series of rejections that come before the positive answer we seek. The sequence is "No, no, no, no, no, no, no, no, no. Yes." And the sooner we get going, the sooner we get to "Yes."

In getting appointments the most common place to encounter a "no" is with a secretary. Many secretaries perceive that part of their job is protecting their boss from intruders. This is important to recognize and it is also important to know that secretaries are generally sensitive to power and authority.

Using this knowledge, here is how your telephone conversation with a secretary might proceed:

You: May I speak with Mr. Jones, please.

Secretary: May I say who is calling?

You: My name is _____ _____.

Secretary: May I tell Mr. Jones what this call is about? (trying to protect boss.)

You: Mr. Smith, the vice president at Consolidated Industries, suggested that I call (use of authority to break through barrier). May I speak with Mr. Jones, please?

Secretary: (sometimes) I'm sorry, Mr. Jones is in a meeting. Could I have your number and I'll ask Mr. Jones to phone you back? (often a rejection.)

You: (keeping the initiative, and the power) I know that Mr. Jones is a busy man. Could you suggest a time when he might be free and I'll phone back?

Secretary: Perhaps after four....

Usually your conversation with a secretary will be easier than this one, and occasionally more difficult. The words above can be the basis for a script, using words you are comfortable with. Until the process is easy for you, I suggest you have such a written script before you when you pick up the phone. Even better, practice the phone call with a friend (back to back, so there is no eye contact) until it becomes natural.

Sometimes a secretary will press you about the purpose of your call. A response like "I need some information from Mr. Jones and need to speak with him in person" will usually work. Always be honest and always remember that your goal is to get an appointment, nothing more.

You might want to call an organization where you have no contact at all; in this situation the best approach is to start at the top. Telephone the president's office and ask the president's secretary for the name of the person to contact for the information you want. Then, when this person's secretary asks the purpose of your call, you say, "Mr._____'s (president's last name) office suggested that I call." Being sensitive to power relationships, the secretary is unlikely to block you any longer for fear that she might be putting her boss's job (or her own) in jeopardy. The secretary respects the authority of the hierarchy and you get through.

Once past the secretary, if there is one, your objective is to get an appointment with your target person.

To achieve this goal, you need to accomplish four things. First, you need to identify yourself. Second, you need to establish that the person with whom you are making the appointment is, as you thought, someone who is qualified to give you helpful information. Third, you need to give this person a reason to see you. And finally, you need to agree on a time and place.

In this first contact you do *not* want to impress this person with how much you know and you do *not* want to get into a discussion of your work experience—avoid being interviewed over the telephone. What you do want is to get the appointment as quickly and as professionally as possible, say goodbye, and hang up.

Once you get to the person with whom you want to meet, your conversation might go like this:

Target
Person: Jones here.

You: Good morning (afternoon), Mr. Jones. This is _____
_____ and I am calling because Mr. Smith at Consolidated Industries told me that you are one of the most knowledgeable men in the industry when it comes to public relations. (You identify yourself and seek to establish the qualifications of your target person.)

T.P.: Ah yes, Frank Smith. How is the old son of a gun?

You: Just fine, Mr. Jones. And, as I say, he spoke quite highly of you. The reason I am calling is because I would like to learn more about the public relations program in your company. Could we meet to discuss this? (You give the person a reason to see you and ask for a meeting.)

T.P.: (if he is being difficult) May I ask why you want to learn more about public relations?

You: (prepared!) I am considering working in public relations, based on a review of my skills and experience, and I am talking to a number of organizations to learn more about the field. Your firm is a leader in public relations, I am told (a little flattery is OK) and meeting with you is very important for the research I am doing. Would you have perhaps thirty minutes late next week? (You attempt to make an appointment and end the conversation.)

T.P.: Perhaps Thursday afternoon . . .

You: That would be fine. At three?

T.P.: Sure. Three is fine.

You: I'll be there, Mr. Jones. To confirm, my name is _____
_____ and the phone where I can be reached during the day is __ __. I look forward to meeting with you in

90

your office next Thursday, the ____ (date) at three pm. See you then. Goodbye.

A teacher of mine once told me something that applies to getting appointments. He said that the two most powerful sentences in the English language are, "I have a problem" and "I need your help." This sounded gimmicky when I first heard it, but I tried his approach and it worked magnificently, and I think I know why. When I say "I have a problem" I am acknowledging the humble truth as I rarely do. And when I say "I need your help" I am once again being truthful, and asking in an unfamiliar and direct way. Such powerful communication has a magical effect on others.

In getting appointments you could do a lot worse than saying "I have a problem" (I need information) and "I need your help" (will you meet with me?).

There are people who will turn you down, but not many. Most people who are successful in this world have gotten that way because, at least part of the time, they are cooperative and helpful. Most people will help if you ask. You will have the best luck if you are absolutely sure that what you want at this stage is information and not a job (yet). After all, you do not yet have sufficient data to commit to a particular job or career. If you are not sure in your heart that you want information, those you approach will pick this up and be less likely to see you.

And even if you do get a few rejections using the approach described here, you will get far, far less than if you went out with your hat in your hand and asked the threadbare "You don't have a job, do you?"

Research Meetings

"Preparedness is the key to success," said General Douglas MacArthur, and this advice applies to research meetings as much as it does to military engagements.

In preparing for success you have already taken one of the most significant steps—you have made an appointment with a person who has information you want. This is a substantial accomplishment.

In preparing for the meeting itself, think in terms of two kinds of information to be collected: information through observation, and information through interrogation. You will recognize the areas for observation, which appeared in similar form earlier. If this seems repetitive, and it is, just remember the importance of alertness. Use all your senses:

- *Your eyes* gather hundreds of clues from the work environment you enter. Is the atmosphere formal, or is it casual? Is it organized, or is it in disarray? Are there rows and rows of work tables, or are the work places individualized? Are people focussed on their work or are they killing time? Even the bulletin boards have messages! A sign "The next S.O.B. who takes my electric drill gets his hand chopped off" communicates powerfully.

- *Your ears* also gather important data. Is the decibel level uncomfortably high? Is the "silence deafening?" Or does the noise level seem about right? Do you hear people shouting at one another, or are voices modulated? Do you hear anger, or do you hear affection?

- *Your senses of touch, smell, and taste* can also collect worthwhile information from the work environment. Do you feel dust and grime on work surfaces or does everything feel clean? Do you encounter pleasant smells or do you find that the smell of the place takes a few minutes getting used to? If food is processed or served, you should ask to taste it and see how it appeals to you.

Although you will probably not want to write down in advance the areas to observe, it is important to make notes immediately after each meeting on any of these observations which seem significant to you. Your goal is collecting information, and this data is important.

The second major source of information is through interrogation—the questions you ask and the responses you get from the person with whom you meet. When I prepare for a meeting like this, I write these questions down in advance. My discussion guide would look like this:

Work done here

- How much with data? with people? with things?
- How much physical? how much mental?
- How much repetitive? how much discontinuous?
- How much managing other people? how much doing the work itself?
- How much writing? how much talking? how much with others?
- How much here? how much away? how much out of town? how much out of the country?

People who are successful here

- Background? training? education? previous experience?
- Personalities which work? introverts vs. extroverts? detail people vs. generalists? team players vs. individualists?
- Skills needed here? (probe) skills which might help? skills which would be wasted?

What about this particular organization? (or group, or department, or division, or branch)

- What are your goals and objectives? how are you doing on them?
- What are you doing well? what are your successes? what are you most proud of?
- What are your particular challenges? (What you really want to know is their identified *problems*, because unsolved problems are what create jobs. If the person you are meeting with seems candid and cooperative enough, you might ask directly about problems at this point.)
- What training is available here? chances to learn? chances to advance?

What about this group of organizations? (or industry)

- How does this organization fit in with others like it? where does it rank? what is the direction for this group? what are the trends?

Anything else you think I should know? (safety net question)

- *Last question: (important!)* Could you give me the names of three people who do work like yours in other organizations? (When you get this information you are networking, expanding your capacity to make more contacts and get more information, *and* you demonstrate to the person you are meeting with that you are truly on an information search and if he is not careful one of his alert competitors might make you a job offer you can't refuse.)

Your particular discussion guide will vary from this and may have less questions (there is no way all the areas above could be adequately covered in thirty minutes.) A good way to remember what you want to ask is to take your list into the meeting with you and a good way to do this, I have found, is to carry a 9" X 12" vinyl folder of the kind most stationery stores sell for under five dollars. There are versions of these folders attractive enough to carry into any meeting and most people are flattered when you ask if you can make notes of their responses. When you open your folder you see blank paper on which to record answers and on the facing side, lo and behold, there is your discussion guide ready to help you if necessary, but out of view of the person you are talking with. Preparation pays off once again.

Meetings have parts just like operas or baseball games. People who are successful in meetings know what is supposed to happen next and I suggest you prepare for this format in your research meetings. First, there is a connection-building part, where you find areas of mutual interest and relax with each other. Then comes the discussion based on the questions above. Finally there is closure when you get three additional names and say thank you and goodbye.

Another area for preparation is your appearance. Everyone from Amy Vanderbilt onward has offered advice on having your shoes shined and suit ironed and this is all worthwhile. The part that advice givers cannot help you with is the dress which is appropriate for the work environment you will be entering. If you will be talking with a blacksmith you do not need to dress in your Sunday best, and if you will be visiting a business office you do not want to look like you are heading for the forge. If you are in doubt about appropriate attire for a particular work environment, ask someone who works there. Or, better yet, go there in person a day or two in advance and check it out for yourself. You can get loads of information by riding up and down on the elevators a few times.

"Remember," a personnel manager wrote recently, "the person doing the interviewing figures you are dressed as neatly and carefully as you ever will be."

A final area for preparation concerns time. A legendary coach of the Green Bay Packers professional football team asked his players to keep "Lombardi time," which meant being there ten minutes early. In all your work-related meetings it is essential to be on time. After all, what is more important? A good way to do this is to keep "Lombardi time" and use that extra ten minutes to catch your breath and review your discussion guide or, on that rare occasion when you have misplanned, the time can be used to get through that traffic jam, find that elusive parking spot, or retrace your steps when you have gone to the wrong floor.

As you gain experience you will find which of these guidelines are most important for you. These meetings are training for the pre-employment interviews to follow and the practice you get here will help you again and again on your careercycles.

After the Meeting

The first thing to do after a research meeting is to find a place where you can make notes and record everything relevant from the meeting that you did not write down earlier.

These notes become an important resource, especially if you later return for pre-employment interviews.

The second thing to do after the meeting is to write a thank you note. *Always* do this, not because you are polite and properly brought up (which I am sure you are), but because it gives you another contact with a significant person, part of your network. It gives this person your address and phone number—which is *very* important if someone calls a week after your meeting and asks if this person knows of someone with your skills—and it also shows that you know how to write.

The third thing to do after your research meeting is to get ready for the next one. Phone the three contacts, using the approach suggested earlier in this chapter. Keep your momentum going. Keep the information flowing in until you get the answers you need and your level of confidence rises to the point of commitment.

It is commitment, the point of power and the point of no return, that we examine in the next chapter.

6

COMMITMENT: MOMENT OF POWER

Concerning all acts of initiative and
creation, there is one elementary truth,
the ignorance of which kills countless
ideas and splendid plans: that the moment
one definitely commits oneself, then
Providence moves, too. All sorts of
things occur to help one that would never
otherwise have occurred. A whole stream
of events issues from the decision,
raising in one's favor all manner of
unforeseen incidents and meetings and
material assistance which no man could
have dreamt would have come his way.

W. H. MURRAY

If you do not work, you are dead.

THE TALMUD

"Amazing how it all pulled together, how the pieces fell into place," the recent career changer was enthusing, "once I made up my mind." For this young woman, the decision made all the difference. The same can be true for us.

Commitment is a simple concept. It is clear and easy to understand and appears in words and action around us continually. Yet behind the simplicity lies the enormous complexity of how commitment happens, what it takes for each of us, and the role commitment—or the lack of it—plays in our lives.

Commitment, the third phase of six in the careercycle, is the point where power becomes concentrated into the energy required for action.

Foundation for Commitment

The precursor for commitment is planning. Out of exploration comes a sense of direction, a certain clarity about the future. When these fruits of exploring are written down and organized, they become a plan. This plan, as an expression of all we can articulate about our future, becomes the foundation for commitment.

Planning is the subject of numerous books and courses and there are as many approaches to the art as there are experts. One of the simplest and best planning techniques is to ask the newspaper person's questions: who? where? when? how? and why? Applied to the work part of your life, here is how these questions might be asked:

- *Who* do I want to work with? What kinds of people, with what kinds of interests and values and beliefs? How many of them do I want to work with? How closely? In what kind of relationships?
- *Where* do I want to work? City, suburbs, or country? Big place or little place? Traveling or staying put? In the factory or in the office? In my home or somewhere else?
- *When* do I want to work? Regular hours or just when the work needs doing? Full time or part time? All year round or just certain seasons?
- *How* do I want to work? At an intense pace or a leisurely pace? With supervision or on my own? Doing repetitive work or doing original activities much of the time?
- *Why* do I want to work, for what purposes? To make the world better or to make money (or some combination of the two)? To create great works or to make new friends?

In answering these newspaper person's questions, you create the major objectives of your worklife. You can then add a time dimension, identifying whatever time periods are involved in your getting what you want. You can also, if you are so inclined, add details on how you intend to execute your plan: what you think you are going to do next, what after that, and so on. At the end of all this, you have a plan that can cover the back of an envelope or several hundred pages.

If you would like a different approach to life planning, there is a one-sheet plan which incorporates most of the traditional planning described above and introduces significant new data. This plan is called a *mind map*.

The mind map can be an excellent addition to the atlas containing the careercycle map and related smaller maps which are found in this book. The mind map can also be a creative and useful bridge from exploration to commitment. The mind map can integrate the newspaper person's questions and much, much more. Finally, the mind map can be helpful to you not only in planning your work life, but in creating the full arc of your life.

What is a mind map? A mind map is a large sheet of paper containing your hand drawn perceptions of where you will go from here with your life. Besides showing the paths and channels that you see yourself traversing in coming months and years, the mind map may contain detailed answers to the newspaper person's questions and exhaustive lists of various kinds.

To create your mind map, locate a piece of newsprint size paper (I use 19″ X 24″) and a large, flat working space. Get pencils, colored pens, and broad tip marking pens. In the center of the paper, draw a small circle which represents you at this moment (resist the temptation to make "you" large—that's another exercise). Then, like spokes leading out from a hub, draw the major currents of your life: your mainstream work, your avocations, the work you may be testing as a volunteer, your educational plans (ending somewhere soon in a degree?), your exercise and play plans, your travel plans, and even the parts of your life which represent the unfolding of relationships. Label each stream and its relevant parts and tributaries and off-shoots, but don't take time to write extensively about your mind map at this point. Fill in as much of the picture as you can visualize, with activities closer to the center representing those likely to happen soon, and with the activities further away representing your long-term plans. Figure 7 shows a simple mind map (yours will be different).

Once you have completed the basic drawing, go back and add whatever questions or comments or lists seem appropriate to you. See what has been stirred up in you by this exercise, and make notes. You might even decide to write several pages of narrative, describing what is going on in this mind map.

When you look at your mind map, notice which streams seem larger, which smaller. Which seem more urgent? Which seem most developed? Which seem less finished? Which seem vague? Look at the mind map in the illustration and try to imagine where that person is in their life.

Even better, show your mind map to a friend. Tell your friend what you see in it and ask for feedback. What does your friend see happening? What seems most important? Seeking help like this gives you another perspective on your life *and* strengthens your support network.

One reason the mind map is such a powerful tool is that it integrates linear left brain function and creative right brain input. The traditional planning approaches emphasize the former. The mind map allows for as much of this left brain input as you want, but through the artistic and graphic elements also opens a large door for messages from the intuitive right brain. The mind map is also a powerful way to check in with yourself, to get a clearer sense of where you are and lay the groundwork for commitment. Like many of the exercises in this book, the mind map can be drawn again whenever you want to clarify your direction.

How Commitment Happens

As noted earlier, the root word of *commitment* is the Latin "mittere" meaning to send. This is an action word, a signal that something is going to happen. Because action has different implications for each of us, commitment happens differently for different people.

FIGURE 7. An adaptation of a mind map done by a twenty-seven-year-old graphic artist and word processor operator, reflecting a future full of work, play, learning, and relationships. You do *not* need to be an artist to create a mind map!

For some, commitment seems spontaneous. It seems to happen with no forethought and no deliberation (and no work and no pain). As one successful career changer told me, "I switched from being a dental assistant to a consultant on a lark."

For those of you who have spent time in earlier chapters pondering discontent and actively exploring options, this may seem like cavalier treatment of a critical life decision. In fact, the career changer quoted above went on to say, "I didn't know I was going to have to rearrange my whole head —it drained all of me until I was worse than empty." This woman is now fulfilled in her career as consultant and her success reflects, I think, the sometimes unconscious pondering and preplanning which usually precedes apparently spontaneous commitment. Generally, we learn how to be right.

A variation of spontaneous commitment is reflected in the senior business executive who told me, "I made up my mind that I was going to do something different," and then went on to do it. This man told me that he had never in forty years as a senior manager sought out a new job or new career. People with jobs, sometimes in dramatically different fields, had always sought *him* out. What he didn't add was that he had a magnificent network of friends and admirers, ranging from members of Congress, to academic leaders, to business executives abroad. This network continually fed him information and opportunities and contacts with those who could offer him new ways to use his skills.

However spontaneous the commitment, proper groundwork increases chances for success.

Sometimes the career decision appears nearly spontaneous, but not quite, as illustrated in this story:

> I was working for this medium size advertising agency in the city and doing well. I ran the department where we did "mechanicals," the final artwork for ads which run in magazines and newspapers.

Though my department was doing fine, the agency wasn't. The day we lost our biggest account I got the axe. It was a Wednesday, I remember, and I was devastated. We had a small party planned for Saturday night and when I got home I told my husband we'd better cancel. I was in no shape for parties.

My husband was very supportive and then he said, "Why not let the invitations stand, but change the theme of the party into 'Let's get Louise (not her real name) a job.' "

For some reason I went along. We ended up with newsprint taped to every wall, full of ideas. By the end of the evening we decided that I should start my own firm in the city specializing in doing mechanicals. We even came up with a name, "Mechanical Marvels" and it stuck.

That was five years ago and the new company is not so new any more. I never looked back. I can't remember being happier.

Although Louise's decision seems to have been made in the four days from Wednesday to Saturday, can you see how it was based on a lot more? Working with mechanicals was right for Louise, based on several years' success, but the volatile atmosphere of the advertising agency was wrong. She was sure that she liked doing mechanicals and she liked working in the city. She just needed a new vehicle and her own firm was it.

Louise is also a positive example for us because of how she involved those close to her—her husband, and then her friends. People who know us provide a useful check on our own perceptions and, as in Louise's case, offer ideas, support, even valuable contacts.

The examples used here illustrate how our values, interests, and skills lead to commitment. More specifically, our values, interests, and skills are the underpinnings for the goals we set for ourselves. And decisions on goals lead to commitment.

The process itself can be seen as a narrowing of options as we get more and more information, and our level of confidence rises. Seen graphically, as in Figure 8, this looks like a river at a point where the channel narrows and the water velocity accelerates.

At the top of this mini-map we have a wide range of options. Usually we first look at these options because discontent in one form or another makes us consider change in our work lives. As we begin to explore, we begin to narrow options. We notice, perhaps, that our values and interests lead us away from social services. As we begin outer exploration, we may decide that although our skills qualify us for dishwashing, that is not what we want.

Because each of us is different, the point of decision and commitment comes at different places on this mini-map. Some of us make decisions faster than others. Some of us require more evidence than others to be sure of the next step. Some of us like more reassurance from those whose opinions we respect. But at some point, if we persevere, we come to the point where we know just where we want to go. We commit.

FIGURE 8

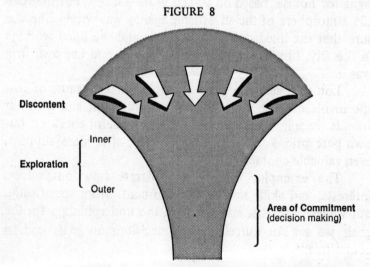

Discontent

Exploration

Inner

Outer

Area of Commitment
(decision making)

Decision makers come in all sizes and shapes but one way to organize decision-making approaches, adopted from Anna Killer-Tiedeman, is presented below as eight different categories. The first four are essentially spontaneous, involving little or no rational thought:

- The *intuitive* strategy is for those who decide on unspoken feelings, because "it feels right."
- The *fatalistic* strategy is for those who leave the decision up to the environment or to fate. "Whatever will be, will be."
- The *compliant* strategy is used by those who go along with others. "If it's OK with you, it's OK with me."
- The *impulsive* strategy is used by those who tend to accept the first alternative presented. "Decide now, think later" is the motto for this category.

Three strategies which put off decisions until tomorrow are:

- The *paralytic* strategy, in which the decider knows he should act but just can't get it done.
- The *agonizing* strategy, in which the decider has so much data and so many alternatives that he wails, "I can't make up my mind!"
- The *delaying* strategy, which says "I'll think about it tomorrow" and hopes new data will come floating in or the need to decide will disappear.

The recommended strategy, the one you will be using if you follow the guidelines presented in this book, is the *planned* strategy. This is a thoughtful approach, using rational processes and integrating emotional and intuitive input. This is a conscious decision-making strategy, used by those who know the value of commitment.

The woman who took an office skills course that led to a professional position as an editor said, "I resolved to be on course by age forty." She was. Her resolve, backed by serious and thoughtful exploration, brought her to the commitment point and success.

Strategies range from those who decide by using all their resources (like us), to those who decide on the spur of the moment, to those who seem to take forever. These are people who prompt letters which begin, "Dear Abby, Joe is a fine man but we have been engaged for twelve years now and he still won't set a date. . . ."

In decisions about careers a cautious, methodical approach may just represent the style of a particular individual, or it may reflect some kind of block. In Chapter Four we saw a man deal with a "not good enough" block and a woman work on a block created by her felt need to continually serve others. Blocks come in all sizes and shapes and, if we are sufficiently motivated, they can be dealt with.

Motivation, of course, is the other area to examine when there is a reluctance to commit. Perhaps there is not sufficient discontent. Perhaps the discontent is mostly talk, and talk that has become so ingrained that it would be hard to give it up. What in the world would we do if there were nothing to complain about?

When motivation is lacking, there usually hasn't been sufficient exploration to form the basis for commitment. Exploration takes motivation and energy, and some would prefer not to extend themselves this way. This is fine, certainly, if this is right for the individual. But look what is missed!

What Commitment Brings Us

In 1938 a senior business executive and insightful management theorist named Chester Barnard wrote:

To try and fail is at least to learn; to fail to try is to suffer the inestimable loss of what might have been.

When we fail to commit we risk "the inestimable loss of what might have been." We give up some piece of ourselves, some part of our potential for being all that we can be.

When we commit, by contrast, we accept the challenge to go for the best. We may not achieve the best, but at least we have tried.

I remember clearly the goal I set as a high school sophomore to run the half mile in two minutes and twelve seconds, which is not *that* bad considering all the clinkers on the cinder track at our little school in Ohio. It was not until the end of my senior year, on a day when I made up my mind to achieve my goal, that I finally did it. In fact, I exceeded my target time by four seconds and demonstrated for myself that I could have been aiming higher.

By contrast, my goal of a year later to make first string on my college basketball team never was achieved. And the truth is that I still feel some remorse about that these many years later—a price I pay for my commitment. However, in striving for my goal I did make the team, and in the process made some good friends and showed myself what I could do. There is not a doubt in my mind that without my initial commitment, which I regret not at all, none of those valuable benefits would have come my way.

I recently heard a quotation attributed to Leo Burnett, the founder of one of America's great advertising agencies: "If you reach for the stars at least you won't end up with a handful of mud." Commit, and go for the best in you.

Not far from here lives a businessman friend who years ago started a fishing lure business, which failed, and then a company to make a unique warning light for emergency vehicles. That failed, too. Then, after lots and lots of little failures, my friend developed a device to help swimming pool owners. That succeeded, eventually, in a big way. But this engaging and enquiring man, now in his fifties, has made a new commitment: to revolutionize the way power boats are driven. I, for one, have absolutely no doubt that he will do it.

An academic colleague of mine recently took a leave of absence to work full time in business management, an activity she finds far more stimulating than the classroom (where she has been a success for years). She loves her new job and they love her. She explored business; then she committed and commitment makes the difference.

When we commit, "all sorts of things occur to help one," according to the W. H. Murray quotation at the head of this chapter. What more could we ask?

Commitment is making a decision, an irrevocable decision that we can change tomorrow (but rarely do). While there are many decision-making styles, with myriad courses and books on the subject, the end result of all decision making is the same: commitment.

Commitment brings us power and it brings results. And commitment can have a profound effect on those around us.

How Our Commitment Affects Others

"No man is an island," John Donne wrote, and the connection becomes clear when we commit.

If we view the impact of our commitment like the ripples spreading out from a stone thrown into a pond, the first to be affected are those with whom we are most intimate: our mates, family, those with whom we live. These special people may benefit most from learning through our commitment just where we stand. If we are willing to communicate clearly to those closest to us, our commitment has its first impact there.

When those closest to us know the direction we intend to take, they are able to serve and support us. When I made it clear that I was committed to writing this book, I got all sorts of help and support: ideas to refine the basic concepts of the book, offers to help with editing, suggestions on publishers, and more. If I had kept silent, none of this assistance would have appeared. The penalty for not communicating is illustrated in the sad story of the senior business executive who is fired but is afraid to tell his wife, and so drives off every morning at the usual time on his way "to work." He drives aimlessly all day, suffering alone, as he sees it (Donne might see it differently).

Our commitment can benefit those closest to us in several ways. For starters, it is just plain more interesting to live with someone who knows where they are going. Commitment usually brings power and enthusiasm, which can be nice traits to live around. Another eventual byproduct of commitment is often material: money flowing in again, money flowing in larger amounts, new travel experiences, new social opportunities. You could make your own list of such benefits, I am sure.

As the ripples spread further from the impact of our commitment, those who help us are affected. One career changer told me how a teacher helped, once she knew what she wanted. "He gave me the courage, the support," she said, "and even referred me to a job near here; he really gave me a boost." This woman found that she had more power, in the form of unanticipated aid, once her direction became clear.

Teachers, counselors, and unofficial helpers like neighbors who are managers or business owners all become potential supporters once we commit. We give out clear signals, perhaps even "I have a problem and I need your help," and the many people who get satisfaction from helping others suddenly join our team. We initiate. They respond.

A special kind of helper is the mentor. A mentor (the word means "faithful counselor" in ancient Greek) is someone willing to form a special giving relationship with us, drawing on their broader experience. The contemporary conception of a mentor is someone in our same organization, but for the traveler on the career cycle this is not necessarily so. One career changer had an informal mentor relationship with a senior executive in a related firm:

> Pierre has been very supportive. He met me across the Bay and told me how to launch a career in our field. He gave me a list of firms in our field.
>
> Later he wrote a testimonial letter for me, to put in with my letters to prospective employers. He was just what I needed.

In my own career journey a cousin, several years my senior, has been a kind of a mentor. I feel comfortable asking him for advice and do sometimes. He once told me, "Anyone will help you if you're willing to ask." Sound familiar? That is valuable direction from a valuable mentor which came to me once I commited.

The more traditional mentor also plays a crucial role in career planning. The president of a multinational corporation with several billions of dollars in sales recently told me this story:

> In the late '50s I saw that you had to be here twenty years to make a substantial decision. So I decided to leave. I had even sold my home.
>
> There was this very bright guy in the company at that time, a fellow considerably senior to me. He could really cut through it. He has high intelligence combined with complete integrity: he says what he means and he means what he says.
>
> Anyway, this guy called me in and told me they had this new job for me in the company. So I stayed and I've done all right. If I was starting all over again, though, I'd do my own business. That's the ultimate test.

This thoughtful executive changed jobs within his company (he has now been there for thirty-two years) and ended up at the top. The support of a mentor, as you can see, was crucial.

All of those affected so far are members of our support system, the network we are using, and as the ripples spread from the impact of our commitment, new members are added to this special group. As we start to explore the outer world we may add a research librarian or someone we have met at a party. The clarity which comes from commitment attracts people. As we explore further, we add some of those with whom we conduct research meetings. Once they know the direction we are heading in they become, to one degree or another, part of our support system. Eventually the force of our commitment spreads beyond the point where we can be personally aware of all those helping us, all those who are part of our network.

Empowerment is the subject of this book, on some level, and when our own power, focussed through commitment, is magnified by the power of those in an expanding network, we are truly empowered. Vector theory in engineering says that when forces which have been pulling in different directions all begin to pull in a single direction, the result is an enormous increase in power. Our commitment, and the support of others, produces such a result.

Impact on the World

R. Buckminster Fuller, who was cited earlier, said:

> ... You do not belong to you. You belong to the universe. The significance of you will remain forever obscure to you, but you may assume you are fulfilling your significance if you apply yourself to converting all your experience to the highest advantage of others.

We cannot fully know our impact on the world. Bucky decided years ago to work "for everyone." Each of us makes a difference in this world and when we commit ourselves we make the decision to go for the best that is in us. We trust, as Bucky suggested, that our impact fits in the greater scheme.

Commitment is powerful because it leads to action. The action for those of us on the career cycle is an opportunity to create change in our work life, as we shall now see.

7

CHANGEPOINT: MOMENT OF TRUTH

Two monks walking down the street
pass an unusually attractive young woman.
The first expells a sigh of desire
and then, sensing that his companion
has noticed, exclaims, "Of course, I don't
want what I want!"

APOCRYPHAL STORY

The more you know about the job, the more
you'll know how to put yourself across.

EXECUTIVE RECRUITER

What is work? and what is not work? are
questions which perplex the wisest of men.

BHAGAVAD GITA

"It was absolutely horrible in the beginning," said the career changer described at the end of Chapter Two. Almost all of us, like the hero, go through a passage of intense emotion at the point of change. It may be horror, fear, guilt, remorse, doubt. More likely, it is some combination of these emotions . . . and more.

This chapter will look at events leading to changes in our work lives, at the changepoint itself, and at events likely to ensue. Mileposts will be identified and suggestions made for moving ahead to the uplifting experiences awaiting us.

Where Are We?

The traveler on the careercycle comes to the halfway point after passing through the commitment phase, a place 180 degrees from the starting point. A look at the careercycle map shows us to be passing through the bottom of the circle described in Figure 9.

This point of change comes after we commit, after we search out the information necessary to arrive at a firm and clear decision on our direction. Commitment provides the emotional energy required to sustain us through the stress of the changes ahead.

The point of change itself, coming in time between commitment and renewal, involves shifts in the way we think and feel and, ultimately, in where and how and why we do our work. All life involves change, and the difference here is that this is major change, entered into consciously.

Change itself is followed by an avalanche of emotions and, before long, by a sense of euphoria we call renewal. Change is rarely easy, on either ourselves or those around us, and the emotions produced by change are powerful and often confusing. Sometimes, in fact, the intensity of the emotions at the moment we are in them makes naming them impossible.

FIGURE 9

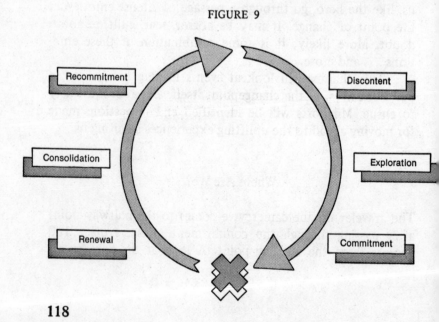

In the Hero's Journey, described in Chapter Two as the genesis for the careercycle, the bottom of the cycle is the supreme ordeal. At this moment of crisis the hero gets what he came for. His reward gained, the hero begins his return with the elixir, or boon, that restores the world. With the career changer, as with the hero, this point of transformation takes many forms.

Many Faces of Change

The point of change is different for each of us and, although there are many common features, there are as many ways of changing as there are people. Here is the story of one career changer:

> When I got out of school, I joined a Big Eight accounting firm. About the time I knew I'd be a partner, I decided to leave. I didn't like big organizations and all that BS and I wanted to be on my own.
>
> I had a wife and two kids, $300 in the bank, and a rented house. I wanted to start my own accounting practice though I didn't have a single client when I quit, and I resolved not to steal clients from my old firm. My old VW was too beat up to let clients see, so I even rented a new car.
>
> In my first year on my own I made twice what I had made working for the old firm. In fact, they passed some of their business my way that first year. What kept me going was that I knew I could always go back to what I was doing before.

In the transition described above the changepoint seems to have come at about the time this man quit his secure job with a national firm. Notice how he remembers several years later the amount of money he had in the bank and the fact that his car and home were rented. That was the place of risk, the place of change. When this same person shifts careers again several years later, the changepoint has a different quality:

> A year later another guy joined me. We formed a partnership. The practice kept growing, but we thought we needed a broader base so we bought out another firm in a small town eighty miles away. Probably a real dumb thing, looking back.
>
> During tax season I'd get up at 5:00 A.M. and deal with my larger clients and then drive up to the other office and do tax returns for retired people and not get home until one in the morning. My partner and I had been looking at houses and land as an investment for a long time. With all that driving I noticed twenty acres for sale in this town I had to drive through to get to our other office. We talked to the owner and got an option to buy the land at what then seemed like a huge price.
>
> We didn't have the faintest idea where we'd get the kind of money needed. We had nothing to borrow against. Then three days before the option expired, we heard about a guy who wanted fourteen of the twenty acres to put up a warehouse on the railroad siding. The deal on the fourteen more than paid for the twenty acres and left us with the other six free and clear.
>
> We put out spaces for fifty mobile homes on our six acres, and although they filled slowly, we were off and running. We did several other land deals and then hired a guy to do the accounting for us. We got so we were doing better than our clients and losing interest—if you're a professional, that's the time to get out.

In both of these changes, this man's high energy and relentless pursuit of options served him well. But in the second change he was more confident and the stakes were larger.

The changepoint came when the fourteen acres were sold on the railroad siding. This time, when the changepoint came, he was ready.

Running a business requires particular personality traits, some of which appear in the example above. For most of us, who end up working in organizations managed by others, the changepoint comes at about the time a job offer is made—sometimes just before, sometimes just after.

In evaluating change when we get to this point on the careercycle, it is crucial to look for other changes in our lives. If we have just lost someone close to us—through death or divorce or even a child going off to college—that represents an important change in our life. Likewise if we have just moved or had surgery or had a large weight loss.

Why do we care about other changes? Each change requires energy—creative energy to adapt to the new situation and sometimes physical energy, like that required to move to a new home. Each of us has a limited amount of available energy and, when we have the choice, we function better when we deal with one major change at a time. When we don't have the choice, we spend some time with a book like this to help with at least part of the change going on in our life.

Getting Job Interviews

In many ways the crucial point on the careercycle comes when we face the person with the power to put our skills to work. This is the job interview, sometimes called the pre-employment interview.

How do we get job interviews?

The most important ingredient for getting to see the person we want is the work we have done to get us to this point. If we have understood our discontent and if we have persevered in our inner exploration, we have started the foundation. And if our understanding of our interests and values and skills has led to exhaustive outer exploration, we have completed the foundation.

The research meetings described in Chapter Five provide interviewing practice that can be had no other way. These meetings *also* provide the data we need to arrive at a point of commitment, of course, but the training in going face-to-face with decision makers is crucial in the job interview phase. If we have built a proper foundation, we are skillful at eyeball-to-eyeball meetings by this time.

If we have had enough research meetings, we now have a clear picture of where to find jobs that are appropriate for our skills and interests. We know who is hiring and who might be hiring soon. We know what these jobs require, what they involve, and what they pay.

If we have had enough research meetings, we now understand what the problems are in the two or three organizations that most interest us. With those we have met, we have defined the challenges that need to be faced and we have a sense of how our skills might do the job.

And if we have had enough research meetings, one or more decision makers in our target organizations have also come to believe that the cluster of skills we offer might just be what they need. We will have, in short, come a long way towards getting our next job.

Sometimes at this point a department manager will say toward the end of a research meeting, "You know, we have a need here for someone just like you." Like any traveler offered sustenance, you value this opportunity. If you are near the point of commitment, you promise to respond soon. If you are at the point of commitment, you say, "Yes, let's talk more seriously."

An excellent way to get to this point with a company is to serve them as a temporary worker, with only a short-term commitment on both sides. This arrangement provides extensive data for both the worker and the employer, the kind of data on which sound decisions are made. If this approach interests you, there is an outstanding book on temporary work, *Working Whenever You Want* by Barbara Johnson, available from Prentice-Hall.

As I write this, a twenty-two-year-old client of mine is being interviewed for a sales position at an insurance company where he started out as a temporary worker. After many research meetings, he was doing temporary work to bring in some income and get more information. His persistence will pay off—this time or next.

This kind of transition from research meeting to job interview is the way this whole process is supposed to happen. When it does, that's beautiful. All your hard work has paid off.

Often, though, you will not get such a specific opening, such a clear invitation. But you will know where the job possibilities are and you know, because you have been doing it, how to approach these organizations. You do this by listing your top job targets along with the contacts you have developed in each organization. You may add other organizations you know about but have not gone to for research meetings. This is your prospect list.

Starting with your top prospect (because you have developed your interviewing skills, you do not need a warmup), telephone the person there with the power to hire you. The appointment-getting approaches described in Chapter Five are the same ones you will use now. You now know how to deal with secretaries; you now know how to ask for an appointment without being interviewed over the telephone. This knowledge will serve you well here.

A recent newspaper ad read, "Amateur job hunting in today's market wastes time, money, and worse . . . it can waste precious opportunities." The ad listed a number to call for "a confidential no-cost or obligation interview with career professionals." Fortunately, if you have followed the path described here, you are no longer an amateur. Moreover, you have discovered by now the enormous power you gain by going out into the marketplace and learning for yourself where best to employ your skills. You now know better than to believe such ads, right?

Preparing for Job Interviews

As the general said, "Preparedness is the key to success." The suggestions made in Chapter Five on how to prepare for research meetings apply here. Your experience with these face-to-face encounters has taught you which preparations are most important for you personally. Two new approaches to preparation, however, might help at this point.

You know by now that a job consists of skills employed to solve problems. So skills are central. And you know from your experience with research meetings that you become more polished with practice. Putting the two together, you might now take some time to practice articulating your skills.

Why practice talking about your skills?

For one thing, almost all of us have been taught not to "brag." We have been told that it is impolite to talk about ourselves, that it is more blessed to listen than to talk. Practice helps us overcome this inhibition. Practice also helps us to clarify our ideas, to organize our presentation in a logical fashion, and to develop relevant, coherent, practical examples to illustrate our skills (memorable examples are essential to effective communication). Finally, practice helps us smooth off the rough edges. The words we will say later in an interview become impressed on our mind and the result is a more natural and believable presentation when we need it.

In a workshop I ran while this book was being written, the participants talked about their skills in front of a TV camera and then saw themselves played back in living color. Each participant chose another workshop member for a one-on-one presentation. Philip, a thirty-six-year-old computer whiz, talked about how his skills at trouble-shooting equipment could be transferred to solving human problems, and learned in the process that he needs to further clarify his career direction. Sara, a twenty-eight-year-old with management skills in human service organizations, wants to use her skills and imminent MBA degree to work in private industry. She learned in this exercise that she is on course and ready for further research meetings.

If you lack access to video feedback equipment, find a friend and practice talking about your skills, using appropriate examples, and then ask for feedback. Both the practice and the feedback will help. And if you can't find a friend, use a mirror and watch yourself perform. Even if you do practice with a friend, the mirror is good for refining your gestures, developing good eye contact, and building confidence.

If you wonder about the value of all this preparation, think back to the last time you met someone new. Do you remember how much of your impression was formed in the first one or two minutes? In workshops I sometimes ask the group to record impressions of a visiting speaker ninety seconds after the talk starts, and then again at the end. There is very little change after the initial impact. First impressions endure.

Here are three magical helpers which will help you create a positive first impression . . . and conduct successful interviews. These magical helpers are proven tools for making persons more powerful.

- *Affirmations* come first. These statements of belief affirm what you know to be true but what some ancient voice in the back of your mind denies. One I used recently was, "I, John, have what it takes to make this an excellent workshop." I repeated this to myself again and again; at first the little voices said, "No way!" and then later, "Well, maybe" and finally, "Sure you do." You might affirm that you have the skills to do a particular job that is new to you. Be sure to include your first name to personalize your affirmation. And be sure to repeat it often enough to get your whole mind programmed the way *you* want it. Rather than thinking about your fears as you drive to an interview, why not try affirmations?

- *Visualizations* come next. With this magical helper, you create an image in your mind's eye of the outcome you want. Perhaps you imagine the person you are about to meet with saying, at the end of the interview, "When can you start?" Make the image as real as possible. Come back to it often. One career changer told me of standing in front of the mirror in his Dallas hotel room and imagining the job offer and then watching himself smiling and saying, "Why, yes, I'd be delighted to join your company." He then walked across the street and got the offer he wanted—and a forty percent pay increase. It all happened, he told me, just as he had visualized.

- *Centering* is the third of the magical helpers available to you in preparing for the job interview. This can be used at any point when you are nervous, but it is especially valuable in the two or three minutes before you walk into the office of the person with the power to employ your skills (remember the impact of the first impression!). Your goal is to return to the calm, solid, true place inside of you, a place you visualize as your "center." Your technique is to deepen and slow down your breathing, to straighten and relax your posture, and to clear your mind of extraneous thoughts. This is an abbreviated version of Transcendental Meditation, which was popular several years ago, and derives from the meditative practices of Eastern religions. It has worked for spiritual seekers for thousands of years and can work for you, too.

These three magical helpers counteract the little voices, heard by most of us, which whisper, "You are not good enough!"

Like Joel in Chapter Four, we restrain ourselves. See if you can identify with this poignant scene from Philip Roth's 1959 novel *Goodbye Columbus* in which the narrator, Neil Klugman, talks to a "little boy" with "the thickest sort of Southern Negro accent" who is entranced by an art book in the library:

"Who took these pictures?" he asked me.

"Gaugin. He didn't take them, he painted them. Paul Gaugin. He was a Frenchman."

"Is he a white man or a colored man?"

"He's white."

"Man," the boy smiled, chuckled almost, "I knew that. He don't *take* pictures like no colored man would. He's a good picture taker...."

Whether we are the "wrong color" or the "wrong sex," "not smart enough" or "not experienced enough," most of us have feelings like those described in this vignette. And most of those debilitating feelings have no more basis in fact than those of the little boy admiring Gaugin.

The human organism is wonderful and mysterious. With all we know about it, my sense is that there is much more that we *don't* know. We do know that these three magical helpers work, and if you call them to your assistance, you increase your chances for having the kind of job interview you want.

Conducting Job Interviews

What is the biggest mistake job applicants make? Here is the opinion of a bank personnel officer:

They expand on their answers more than they should. They tell too much concerning personal matters not relating to the job. It's a sign of nervousness and being overeager.

Your experience in meeting with people, and the three magical helpers, will give you an edge in dealing with "nervousness and being overeager." But what about expanding on your answers too much? And what about telling too much about personal matters? If you have read this far you will have a sense of the answer. It boils down to strategy.

You have done the inner exploration needed to get you into research meetings. You have gathered enough data to make a commitment. Now you have made an appointment for a job interview and have prepared yourself to be successful. The last step is to develop a strategic plan.

The foundation for your plan is an understanding of the lay of the land, a knowledge of the territory. Historians say that Wellington walked the Belgian fields at Waterloo planning each piece of the engagement a full eighteen months before he met Napolean there. You, too, will profit by knowing the battleground.

The territory covered in most job interviews can be seen as having four parts:

- *Connection building* starts just about any kind of interview. This occurs in the first few moments where old friends make eye contact and move on, if they are rushed, and people with more time talk about sports, international events, even the weather—but always something of mutual interest. The word "rapport" might easily be substituted for "connection," for this first phase is to get you on the same wave length as the other person, and to set you both at ease. Be prepared with some comment, perhaps relating to the conversation which got you the interview or to the attractiveness of the office or to an award on the wall. Keep it low key and look for connections.

- *Preliminary questions* come next. These are questions you use to establish the purpose of the interview and begin moving toward your goal. A common line of questioning at this point might start with you saying, "I understand that this position would involve analyzing financial data . . . ." and move on to define the organization's needs and the problems you are expected to solve. Check out your perceptions and be sure you and the decision maker are on the same wavelength. What is the job title? Is there a job description and, if so, can you have a copy? Where would you work? Who would you report to? Would there be a company car? Travel? Unusual risks or benefits?

- *Pivotal questions* flow from the preliminary questions. These cover issues of substance, the issues that determine whether you want the job and whether they make the offer—and you *do* want the offer at this point. In this phase you review your skills, with examples that relate to this organization, and make sure they register by asking something like, "Would this be appropriate here?" Because you are focussed on solving problems in the organization you are not likely to "tell too much concerning personal matters." You do want to establish the crucial terms of the job now, including compensation. Bring this up if you need to, with a direct question.

- *Closure* is the fourth and final part of the job interview and the place where great things can happen, but too often don't. This is the time when a conclusion is reached; it is tough because one or both participants feel terribly vulnerable. Closure usually requires asking for what you want . . . and risking rejection. Because you have planned for this moment you might ask a general question like, "How do you feel I fit?" Or you could be more direct and say, "I believe I am right for this job. What do you think?" Or you could be less direct and try, "I could start a week from Monday. . . ." (in sales this is called a "minor point close"). Your goal here is to reach a decision, and even if it is to delay, it is better to know it now for, after all, knowledge is power.

Now that you know the territory—connection building leading to preliminary questions leading to pivotal questions ending in closure—and have been over it several times during research meetings, you need to think about how you want to cover it. My suggestion, coming from experience on both sides of the interviewer's desk, is that you plan to be in control the whole way. You think through what you want and are then prepared to make it happen, however uncomfortable that posture may be for you. Be prepared to lead, even though, like a skillful general, you may at times find yourself in retreat.

Control in an interview involves taking initiative. It means being active and asserting yourself. Control in an interview has two parts:

- *Talking* is half of initiating in an interview. This means asking questions, as you have learned to do in research meetings, and it means talking about your skills—collecting the payoff for all the thinking and organizing and rehearsing that has gone into the words you use about your skills. Talking is how you deal with unusual situations like the one I encountered in my early twenties when the owner of a company said, without a word of introduction, "Tell me about yourself," and then shut his mouth and leaned back in his chair.

- *Listening* is the other half of initiating in an interview. Much has been written about "active listening" and certainly you want to incorporate that kind of participation, with probes and encouraging body language and repetition of key points. In the listening phase you are genuinely interested in collecting relevant data, both verbal and nonverbal. You need to know how you are doing. You need to know when to change course, when to give more information, when to ask for more. You will be looking for the moment when an offer is actually made (one reliable indicator is when the interviewer brings up the issue of how much you will be paid). There is lots to listen for and good listeners have plenty of control. Finally, listen for, not against: try the other person's perspective, and notice how much more you hear.

When you exercise control over an interview through both talking and listening, you are using effective communication. You are not one of those a personnel director for a Probation Department was talking about when he said, "You ask them why they are applying for this job and they say they like to work with people; you could do lots of jobs and work with people."

Sometimes you meet with several members of an organization before a job offer is made, a situation which requires only a small shift in strategy. Be sure you know who the main decision maker will be—usually your future boss or that person's boss—and pay special attention to getting a positive response there. With others, find out where they fit in the organization and then present those aspects of yourself that are relevant to their position; for example, if you are talking to the controller, be sure to establish your skills in working with numbers and those who manage them.

Meeting with several people at one time is more complex. Such group interviews can be stressful (I certainly found them so), and yet most of the same principles apply as for any interview. Be prepared. Stay in control. Communicate. Close. With a group try to determine who has the main decision-making power and be sure to make your case there. Be alert to those who seem to support you, and use their enthusiasm to sway any doubters. Make personal contacts, ideally in a one-on-one encounter after the interview, to get the feedback you need and, ultimately, the answer you want.

Finally, there are the interviews that no one could expect. There are "interviewer passive" interviews like the one described earlier where all you get is a "Tell me about yourself." There are "interviewer active" interviews where the interviewer talks incessantly, usually out of nervousness and inexperience, and you need to gently interrupt to register your skills. And then there are freak interviews like the one an English friend told me about, when he was applying for admission to Cambridge University: the Cambridge don who was doing the interviewing spent the entire time on the floor under his desk.

Much ado has been made about resumes, and they deserve a word in this section. To paraphrase F. Scott Fitzgerald, nothing is so overrated as a good resume and so underrated as a good interview. A former student came to me recently seeking job-finding help. He had three attractive resumes, all of which he proposed to revise. As we talked we both saw that he had been putting all his energy into revising words (which he is skillful at) about himself, and no energy getting out to see people who could hire him (which will be harder for him). The main function of his resume was to sustain his procrastination.

When McDonnell Douglas wants to sell a space craft to NASA, they do not run an ad in *Life* magazine. Their space craft is unique, one of a kind, not a package of corn flakes where millions of boxes are the same. So the McDonnell Douglas people meet personally with the decision makers at NASA. You are no less unique than a space vehicle, and you, too, deserve a face-to-face presentation.

After McDonnell Douglas visits NASA they send the appropriate written materials to the appropriate people. They send a thank you note, as you will. They send product specifications, and you also will usually provide information about yourself in a letter, application form, or resume—created just for that firm, if possible.

If, like most people, you want to prepare a resume before your job interviews, make an exercise out of it. Make your resume fifteen or twenty pages long. List *everything* good about yourself that you can think of: all your skills and all your accomplishments. Then review this list before the interview as a reminder of what you want to cover (but do not give it to anyone); you can also use this preliminary resume to prepare whatever material you want to send *after* the interview.

Building Confidence

Hiring people is scary. Confidence reduces scariness. So if you want to get hired, look for ways to help the decision maker's confidence in you grow and grow.

Everything this book has said so far helps build confidence. For one thing, you have built a strong foundation, so *you* are confident. For another, your research meetings have made you more confident, both in your attitude toward decision makers and in your certainty that you are heading in the right direction. All of this builds confidence in the decision maker you face in the job interview. And this confidence moves events your way.

A friend of mine tried for over a year to get hired by a blue chip international marketing company. He found excuse after excuse to come back and ask about the sales job he wanted (his persistence alone must have impressed the local manager!). When he finally got the job interview he sought, my friend concluded with these words:

> Look, if you're hiring me because I'm black I'll sit here all day long and be black as can be. I'll be as black as anyone you can find.
>
> But if you're hiring me because I can sell your product line successfully, then the best decision you can make today is to offer me this job. The only decision you could make that would be smarter would be to hire two just like me.

Not all of us are sufficiently bold and extroverted to make such a speech. Yet this sales executive does offer us a beautiful example of how to inspire confidence.

The way many prospective employers ask to have their confidence built is to express concerns. You might hear, for example, "We're concerned that you don't have the right experience for this job." Our impulse is to take this personally: What's wrong with me! I suggest to you, however, that instead of looking at this as a form of rejection (and it may *feel* like rejection), that you look at this as an appeal from the interviewer to have his or her confidence built.

Appeals for confidence building come in many forms. Some are out front, like concerns expressed about your experience. These can range from too little experience, to the wrong kind, to too much. The way you respond to this is to move to what they really care about: skills. You restate your relevant skills, with appropriate examples, to illustrate that you can solve the identified problems—regardless of the specifics of where you have been and what you have done.

When I was applying for the college teaching job I have now, the Dean expressed concern about my lack of experience in building library resources. I earnestly dredged small pieces from my skills bank which remotely suggested that I could build up a library (in fact, I have been miserable at it), and then recapped the skills I felt were essential to solving the *real* problems of the position. Afterward I realized that what the Dean really wanted was to be reassured that he was making the right decision. The library was, and is, a very small part of the job.

Tougher to handle are unspoken reservations. The applicant for the sales position quoted earlier sensed that his race was important and tried to put the issue in perspective. He defused the issue by joking about it. People come to me and say, "I'm too old" or "I'm too young" or "Women never get very far in that company." And I say, "Yes, there is lots of bias in the world against old people, young people, women, gay people, black people, white people, ad infinitum. What is *relevant* is not whether you think you are in one of those categories, but whether you have the skills and the will to do the job." Focus not on some arbitrary identity, but on what you can do.

I read recently about a young woman who was one of four pianists applying for a job at an elegant cocktail lounge. Each of the other candidates let the prospective employer select the music played during the audition. The manager was tired and had one of the first three in mind for the job when Susan sat down to play. "If I saw a lot of people in their twenties in the audience," she told the manager, without being told what to play, "here is what I'd do," and she played a contemporary song.

"If I saw an older group," she continued, "I'd play some of this," and she played a standard. "If the audience seemed quiet or melancholy, I'd play this."

The manager was impressed with her initiative and versatility. Then Susan played her trump card: "And if I looked over at you, and saw you'd had a bad day, I'd play this." She moved into "Smoke Gets in Your Eyes."

"That's my favorite song," said the manager.

"I know," Susan answered. "I asked the bartender." She got the job.

Negotiating

The time between when you get a job offer and when you accept (or reject) it is a rare moment of high power for the prospective employee. The organization has committed. It wants you. And the organization is vulnerable until you say "Yes." Seen graphically (Figure 10), this is a peak of interest that will be exceeded later only if you have an ongoing and successful career in the organization.

Used wisely, the time between the job offer and the acceptance can be very productive. Because of this, it is pru-

FIGURE 10

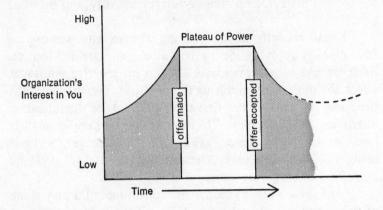

dent to ask for time to consider all but the lowest level jobs. A friend of mine offered a job at a large company blurted, "I don't know what to say," and the senior manager who made the offer responded, "Say yes." When he did so, my young friend abdicated any opportunity to negotiate.

Negotiation of a job agreement involves discovering where the organization has flexibility ... and where you have flexibility.

The most common issue for negotiation is compensation. One book advises that you *always* ask for more than you are offered, but I would temper that. Your research meetings should have revealed what people are being paid for comparable work and if the offer is at that level, and if it meets your needs, then perhaps you do not negotiate salary. What you do negotiate is what is important to you. Is it office location? job title? the kind of company car you are assigned? a productivity bonus? particular working hours? Know what you want and ask for it now. It may be much tougher later.

An organization may lack the flexibility to pay you more money to start, but may be able to increase your salary after three or six months if your work is good. Negotiate that agreement, including the amount, now. An organization may not be able to make you a manager at the start, but might promise such a promotion after a year if your performance merits it. Again, negotiate that now.

By now you must see the importance of getting all this in writing. It is valuable for both sides to have a letter stating the terms of employment, and it is crucial for you to have this before you accept. A salesman I know was once offered a job at what he heard as $1500 a month, but when he got the confirming letter (this was a wise salesman) the pay turned out to be $15,000 a year, some $3000 less than he expected. It happens that he took the job, but you can bet that he had learned the value of getting it in writing.

Negotiate wisely and you will impress your future employer with your skill *and* create the kind of job you deserve.

Pulling Back

Some arrive at the changepoint and then pull back. They may even have the job offer they thought they wanted, yet still they shrink away from making that final crossover, the passage through the changepoint.

A woman I counseled informally spent several months interviewing for senior management positions in nonprofit organizations. She prepared a beautiful resume. She collected impeccable references. She refined her interviewing skills. After several "near misses" in which she was one of two or three finalists, she was offered a well paying position as director of a conservationist group—and turned it down. Like the monk at the head of this chapter, it seems that she did not want what she wanted.

Several months later this woman is doing more inner exploration to sharpen her focus on career direction, and this seems appropriate for her. There are other kinds of pulling back, too.

The career changer described at the start of this chapter, the man who started out with a large CPA firm, came to a workshop I led because for three years he could not get started with work. After he moved on from his own firm, the mobile home park he and his partner bought grew into a number of self-storage locations in three states producing a six figure income for him, even after he was no longer active in the operation.

"I approach the point of actually starting something new," this man told the workshop, "and then I pull back." He wants to pursue his interest in music, and has even built a recording studio in his home, but he just "can't get into it." It developed, as he talked further, that he had spent most of the last three years as a single father caring for his two young children, but that now this situation was changing. He left the workshop committed to taking the first steps to building a new career around his music.

There are lots of ways to pull back, and most of us have the impulse at one point or another. When we pull back, the challenge is to understand why and then do the work we need to do before moving on to whatever comes next.

Moving On

The career changer quoted in the first sentence of this chapter found that his changepoint, his moment of truth, came after he started in his new job. A thirty-three-year-old woman who moved from a publishing house to a bank had a similar experience:

> I accepted the new job and then felt really connected to my old company. I felt guilty. I felt as though I was betraying them, and I had never felt that way before.

Thinking about the bank I worried that they might be right wing, supporting the fascists in El Salvador, and things like that. But I made the change, and once I got started I found that I liked my new work group. Otherwise I might have continued to believe my earlier fears.

Some small voice in most of us cries, "What have I done!" after we change, even as the rational side, the part of us that knows what is true and that is our source of hope, tells us that it is right to move on and that just ahead lies renewal.

8

RENEWAL:
THE HIGH
THAT BINDS

God respects me when I work,
But he loves me when I sing.

RABINDRANATH TAGORE

Unless we foster versatile,
innovative and self-renewing men
and women, all the ingenious
social arrangements in the world
will not help us.

JOHN W. GARDNER

"I'm still very much on a high," said the career changer in Chapter Two, as he talked about his transition from police work to business.

Renewal is the sense of well-being and rediscovered confidence we encounter upon passing through the change-point. This is an especially invigorating part of the journey, where we discover new power, new energy, new life force. It is a natural high available to those who risk their present selves for the sake of their future selves.

In the careercycle, this is the start of the journey home. Renewal begins an upward sweep which takes us back to the top again. Like a horse on his way back to the barn, we have a sense that we are heading in the right direction, and the path is joyful.

Renewal, Reawakening, Rebirth

Each morning when we awake we have a sense of renewal. The awake part of our twenty-four hour cycle is followed by several hours of sleep which restore our energies and freshen our perspective. We are told, "You'll see it differently in the morning," and we usually do.

The ancient celebrations at the time of the winter solstice mark the rebirth of the annual cycle, the point where days once again become longer and spring growth and summer warmth are not far off.

Perhaps more than any other phase, renewal is truly a cyclical phenomenon. The daily cycle of the sun and the annual shifting of the earth's axis are as old as life itself. In human experience the emotional "up" which follows "down" periods is familiar to most of us, and as we come to understand life we see that these mood swings come in cycles.

The experience of renewal can be a profound, once-in-a-lifetime event, like a rebirth. For the traveler on the career-cycle, the person willing to give all, the rewards can be astounding. Reinhold Niebuhr has written:

> The conquest of self is in a sense the inevitable consequence of true self-knowledge. If the self-centered self is shattered by a genuine awareness of its situation, there is the power of a new life in the experience.

New Jobs, New Beginnings

The sense of rebirth that comes from change is both an opportunity and a challenge. In the first hours and days in a new job it is important to build trust, develop sound communications, and start to establish positive relationships with new associates. The opportunity to start anew is a special privilege; the challenge is to make the transition with awareness and sensitivity to those already in this work environment.

The physician whose work on her emotional blocks was described in Chapter Four has now, six months later, made a commitment to photography. Her work is magnificent; she is ebullient and enthusiastic. She has also decided to practice medicine part-time, and is looking at clinics to associate with. She views both of these work areas as new, and brings high, positive energy to them.

The listening and talking skills that you developed during research meetings and job interviews will serve you well now. Spend time with the people around you. Work to understand your new environment. What makes things happen here? Who are the real leaders? What are the unspoken rules and hidden agendae? Make your new beginning the best that it can be.

Take the time and put in the energy to build a solid foundation. Be prepared to give back, because you are getting a lot.

What You Get

Let's be honest about it. There are *lots* of personal benefits from arriving at the renewal stage. There are lots of personal benefits from the exploration and commitment phases, too, but these are usually less obvious at the time. In fact, these stages can be hugely difficult in places. But the renewal time is upbeat and joyful and full of good feelings. It is the pleasure which comes after the pain.

Here are the benefits of this phase described by a recent career changer:

> I found that I got an increase in self-esteem and self-confidence from the process. It gave me a feeling of competence that I like a lot.

There are social benefits from this job that I didn't have when I worked by myself or in my home. I enjoy my time with the people I work with. I also found that I like structure in my life, a clearer separation between work and non-work.

Once you experience a change like this, you want to go back and achieve it again.

The sense of renewal we feel as we enter a new phase of our work life reflects the profound importance of productivity in the human scheme. We are made to work, we need to work, we want to work.

Love also comes to us during renewal. The increased "self-esteem and self-confidence" that come to career changers, like the one above, attract positive feelings from those around us. "Everyone loves a winner," runs the old cliché, and the person who has successfully restructured his or her work is respected and admired (and, yes, some will secretly envy us and some will think we are crazy). As we come to feel better about ourselves, we feel better about others in our life. This growth in positive emotions is very much like what we call love.

The joy of learning is an integral part of renewal. Passing through the changepoint we learn about inner resources we never knew we had. We learn the value of all the earlier learning we did during the discontent and exploration and commitment stages. And we feel the joy and sense of mastery of the learning involved in our new tasks. John Gardner has written:

> For the self-renewing man the development of his own potentialities and the process of self-discovery never end. It is a sad but unarguable fact that most human beings go through their lives only partially aware of the full range of their abilities.

It is exciting to learn that we have abilities we never before knew existed. Like the joy of the child with a new toy, we are stimulated and fully alive as we learn more about ourselves and more about the world around us. Some say that learning is the highest purpose of mankind. Whatever you think about that, I wish for you the ecstasy which can spring from learning.

The first summer I taught at Oxford University, I noticed that I was on an emotional high almost consistently during the eight weeks in England. Pondering this later, I concluded that this feeling came from the almost constant stimulation of new experiences, new data, new learning, new challenges. As I study people on the careercycle, and observe my own experience, I conclude that there is an even greater potential for such high stimulation from changes in our work lives.

What other personal benefits come from renewal? There is powerful satisfaction as we move toward fulfilling our destiny. As we move through the careercycle, we learn more and more about what we are and what we can be. Abraham Maslow talked about this as our highest level need and called it "self actualization." He wrote:

> Even if all these other needs are satisfied, we may still (if not always) expect that a new discontent and restlessness will soon develop, unless the individual is doing what *he*, individually, is fitted for. A musician must make music, an artist must paint, a poet must write, if he is to be ultimately at peace with himself. What a man *can* be, he *must* be. He must be true to his nature.

In each of us is the pull to be all that we can be. We emerge from the changepoint ready to move toward this ideal.

A senior business executive, with several major career changes to his credit, talked in these terms:

They talk about me repotting myself every few years and that analogy is apt. I enjoy changing challenges, changing jobs, changing my environment and it seems to me it's just like a plant in a new location.

I garden when I have the time and I notice that I give the new plants special attention. They get fresh soil and injections of fertilizer. They start to look healthy and flourish. It works for those plants just as it has worked for me.

If plants get healthier during repotting, there is evidence that we human beings do, too. Dr. Alan Cooper, a physician studying relaxation therapy, says, "We often hear how anger and depression are detrimental to health. I believe that the converse is even more true." He continues, "Hope and optimism are gigantic forces in improving health." When we move out from the anger and depression often encountered in the discontent stage, we act to improve our lives, including our physical health. When we are buoyed by the hope and optimism of the renewal stage, we can physically feel that improvement happen.

As the poet says at the beginning of this chapter, "God loves me when I sing." The many benefits that come to us during renewal, some understood and some just sensed, bring us to our work joyful and full of song.

What You Give

Although we get a lot from renewal, the potential is there for giving even more. Consider the inspiration that others may feel from our example. "If he can do it, maybe I can, too." Consider the joy that rubs off on those around us. When we laugh, the world laughs with us, finding our joy contagious. And consider all those who benefit from our using our skills in a more appropriate setting and with renewed energy!

Bosses benefit, co-workers benefit, our friends benefit, the whole world benefits.

As others benefit from our life, they feel attracted to us. This new connection based on reborn energy truly is a "high that binds."

Our perspective shifts once we have passed through a renewal experience. Here are the words of a thirty-eight-year-old woman who has been there:

> When I look at the faces in the workshop I sense that people getting ready to change have no awareness of what it costs interiorly to someone who has changed. It's like they're foreigners, speaking another language. There's no way of talking them into it.
>
> The main value of being here is to remind me, after all the hassles, how easy it is to get lost and how difficult it is to be in transition. It makes me treasure and honor what I've gone through. I have lots of empathy for people who haven't made the jump.

This career changer does not minimize the difficulties of the journey. She comes through with her eyes wide open. And yet she clearly has much to offer, especially to those still poised at the brink of change.

How do others benefit from our renewal?

Look at what the world gains from public figures who survive change and emerge renewed:

- Winston Churchill ascended to the position of First Lord of the Admiralty in World War I but was then discredited by the failure of the Dardanelles campaign and crashed. Churchill's opposition to the appeasement policies of Neville Chamberlain led to his replacing Chamberlain as Prime Minister in 1940—the rest is history. Churchill has achieved a comeback that inspired the world.

- Muhammad Ali made not one comeback but several as he became the world heavyweight boxing champion three times, a record. The power of the inspiration of his rebirth is illustrated by an incident that occurred several months ago: driving in Los Angeles, Ali saw a crowd gathered and stopped. A young man considering suicide was poised atop a tall building, and only when Ali went up to talk with him did he agree to come down. Here again, the power of renewal made a difference in other lives.

- Ronald Reagan, however you may feel about his politics, had a kind of rebirth when he survived an assassination attempt by John Hinckley, Jr. In a television interview not long after, Nancy Reagan said that her husband's perspective had shifted following that experience: he now feels, she said, that his life is no longer his own but belongs, rather, to the people whom he serves.

Although most career changers do not become known around the world, all can have an impact on those around them. Most career changers I see go from being bored, mediocre performers at work to inspired, top performers. This is particularly true if the exploration anticipating the change has been thorough, and the changer has chosen a path which is significantly more in harmony with his or her interests and skills.

Beyond affecting others by doing their work well, career changers can help in a more tangible way: they often become excellent resource persons. Friends and acquaintances who have heard about the change in their work life come and ask, "How did you do it?" The articulate career changer can provide specific tips and valuable how-to advice. The willing career changer can provide access to job resources and names of people to contact. And any career changer can offer a willing ear and the example which says, "You, too, can do it."

Supporting someone is an important, and delicate, business according to this career changer:

Loving someone can give them the energy to jump *and* loving someone can keep them from jumping. I guess the thing is to love them whether they jump or not.

My mentor and partner once said to me, "I have never seen you so close to the edge of knowing that you are good enough, Toni (not her real name), and I want you to know that it is OK if you don't get past that."

The career changer who has been (and will continue to be) supported by a network of friends and contacts earlier in the careercycle now becomes part of a network supporting others. The favor is returned, the debt paid back. When someone calls and asks for a research meeting, do you suppose the career changer could say no? When a friend of a friend asks for names of influential people in the field, do you suppose a career changer would turn her down? When a former associate asks for an honest reference, do you think a career changer would waffle? No way!

Like Daniel Boone, the career changer is explorer become guide. Like Daniel Boone, the career changer has covered the territory, fallen in lots of holes, and come through in one piece. Like Daniel Boone, the career changer can inspire others.

In the Hero's Journey, the adventurer emerges from the supreme ordeal with a boon (the pun is intended) for all mankind, an elixir which heals the world. The traveler on the careercycle likewise emerges at the renewal stage with gifts of enormous potential for those ready to receive them. The elixir of inestimable value is offered up.

Renewal and Renewal

The Zen monk was asked what it is like after achieving enlightenment and he responded, "Mountains are mountains and rivers are rivers." Nothing has changed. No big deal.

At the same time, renewal is essential to life. Joseph Campbell sees it as a countervailing force:

> Only birth can conquer death.... Within the soul, within the body social, there must be—if we are to experience long survival—a continuous "recurrence of birth" to nullify the unremitting recurrences of death.

Renewal is as much a part of the human condition as death, and it is as much a part of work as the well-documented destructive aspects. The challenge for us is to recognize renewal, to understand its value, and to will to achieve it.

Renewal is an integral part of the cycle of work, but the feeling may appear at more than one point as we achieve small triumphs on our journey around. It is also true that our sense of renewal sometimes disappears just as rapidly as it appears. Consider these comments from a twenty-nine-year-old bus driver who was one of 140 laid off recently by a metropolitan transit district:

> When I saw that red bulletin on the board, it was the saddest thing I'd seen in a long time. Before this I was off for a whole year trying to find a good job. When I got this job, I thought I was in heaven.

Sometimes we are catapulted from heaven back to the real world. In terms of the careercycle, we are thrust ahead to the discontent stage much sooner than we expected. The pain is intense, as this bus driver's words tell us, but the traveler on the careercycle knows how to climb out of the dust and get on the path once again.

The renewal time in our work life is a period of high energy, high motivation, and what we often call happiness. If we are alert to what is happening to us, we avoid *hubris*, the overweening pride that comes before the fall. We accept these fine feelings as part of our life. And if we are conscious, we fully enjoy the sense of renewal while it is upon us.

Renewal, however, like all emotionally altered states, cannot last. Before we know it, this high new energy starts to integrate into a consolidation phase.

9

CONSOLIDATION: GETTING IT TOGETHER

At the still point of the turning world.
Neither flesh nor fleshless;
Neither from nor towards;
At the still point, there the dance is.

T. S. ELIOT

That which we call learning is
recovery of our own knowledge.

PLATO

"I always strive for new experiences," said the executive who has repotted himself in several careers. "And there is always some adjustment and trauma." For this man, and for us, the consolidation stage in the careercycle is a time of new experiences . . . and a time of adjustment and trauma.

A sense of renewal lingers into the consolidation period. The high feelings of having made it through the change point turn into a sense of quiet inner pride and self confidence. The stimulation from new dimensions of our work life keeps our days rich and full and interesting.

Yet the many adjustments to new conditions require extra energy. The high of coming through the transition period provides this energy for adjustment, and as the renewal high diminishes, the need for adjustment diminishes, too, and we settle into our new environment. Our new-found energy sustains us through the traumas of change, and then shifts to support us in addressing the problems we came to solve.

At the "still point" of consolidation we assess and evaluate. We consider where we have got to and how this compares with where we were headed. We look at new patterns in our lives—new ways of commuting to work, new relationships with co-workers and bosses and clients, new processes for doing the work itself—and we ponder where these exceed our expectations, and where they fall short.

Consolidation, then, is a place for taking stock while preparing for the journey ahead.

What We Wanted and What We Got

Way back when we were feeling the discontent that led to this change in our work life, we had a vague idea of what we wanted. "If only my boss understood me better," or "I wish I could have more contact with customers," or even "Why doesn't this work excite me anymore? Where has all my motivation gone?" These hazy, half-formed questions were the beginnings of the fantasy that became what we went on to explore.

Exploration sharpened the focus. We looked inward and saw the kinds of values and interests we had and began to get a sense of work environments where these might be shared. We then checked this out in the library and with friends and ultimately with people who were out doing the kind of work we thought we wanted. Once we had explored enough to know that there was something better out there (or elsewhere in our own organization) we made the emotional plunge. We committed.

Commitment crystalized our energy around our new work goal. Commitment is specific, rather than vague, and the specific picture of what we were aiming for shifts some once we get it. Anyone who has run a marathon knows that the image of crossing the finish line is a powerful part of the commitment to complete twenty-six miles ... and that the reality is going to be different from the fantasy.

A central question in the consolidation period is how close together are the image and the eventual reality.

To answer that question, think back to the first conscious steps toward a new work environment. A backward look in the form of a work history review was suggested in Chapter Four. Drawing "my island" was another approach offered. Examining values, interests, and skills is important, too. What did we learn from these exercises about what we want, and how does this compare to what we got? What are the discrepancies? How important are they?

Sensual perceptions are important for most of us. How do we like the way our new environment looks, sounds, smells, tastes? How does this sensate input compare with what we expected? How critical are the discrepancies?

Work is achieved with the skills we apply to achieving work goals, and awareness of our skills is a theme running throughout this book. Are we using the skills we thought we would be using in this new work? Are we using others we had not thought about? Are we deficient in some skill areas? Are we doing what we can to continue to develop our skills? Remember the importance of continuing to learn, keeping in mind these words from Max Planck, when he was awarded the Nobel Prize:

> Looking back ... over the long and labyrinthine path which finally led to the discovery (of the quantum theory), I am vividly reminded of Goethe's saying that men will always be making mistakes as long as they are striving after something.

We keep on making mistakes in our work ... and in our choices of the work we do, and this is an integral part of the process we are immersed in.

"Don't get dissatisfied too easy," said the seasoned executive quoted at the start of this chapter. "Do your work as damn well as you can." No matter how carefully we have done our research, we will find that our new work has not eliminated all our problems. If we had trouble getting up at 6:30 a.m. before, we will probably have it still. If we made mistakes adding columns of figures, we will still make mistakes. If there was continuous friction between us and the boss, we will probably still have boss problems.

We do not change our personality when we change jobs. Problems in us which we have not fully resolved—or which we choose to live with—will still be problems, sooner or later, in our new work. What does happen, if we have done our research thoughtfully, is that our personal foibles are less critical now . . . and our personal strengths are better utilized than before.

As we consider and assess our new position, we come to specific action alternatives.

Managing Work

A whole cluster of actions come under the heading of managing work. Because we have been actively involved in choosing this new work, and because we come here with new energy and expanded insight, we have the power to manage our work life in ways we might not have considered before.

Some think that managing is an activity done only by mature males in business suits. Not true. All of us do management tasks. The question worth considering at this point is how well we do such tasks.

There are many ways to understand the art of management (the best books on the subject are those by Peter Drucker), but the classic four elements still seem relevant. In this traditional view, management is seen as the functions of planning, organizing, leading, and controlling. These are important to us in our work, whether or not we are called "a manager."

Planning is looking into the future, considering where we want to go, and then determining how we intend to get there. As we become more aware of the careercycles in our lives, our planning becomes more relevant. We better understand the base of experience from which we project ahead. We become more realistic in our goals (often while becoming more idealistic in our life view). We become better able to utilize both internal and external resources in reaching our goals.

Organizing is identifying our resources and putting them to use in the manner most likely to achieve our goal. If we have subordinates, organizing includes working out who does what with whom, and when and where. If, like most people, we do not have subordinates, organizing just means getting the most from our personal resources—energies, enthusiasms, interests, skills, experiences, financial reserves, friends, and acquaintances. Organizing is identifying these resources and putting them to work.

Leading is motivating others to do what you want. Those who manage others are expected to lead, though many do it poorly. For the traveler on the careercycle, leadership means inspiring the many people who *can* help us toward providing their help. All of us interact with others, and all of us need to initiate and to enlist the support of these people once in a while.

Controlling is getting data on how we are progressing toward our goal, and then acting on that data. Controlling is not manipulating, as in "He is a highly manipulative person." Controlling, as it applies to the careercycle, means staying in charge. It means claiming our power. It means being flexible, where that is appropriate, and being forceful, when that is required to reach our goal.

How do planning, organizing, leading, and controlling apply to managing our work? The most important place they apply is in creating durable relationships.

Relationships with peers are usually the most critical to success at work (despite the importance many attach to boss relationships). Peers can't be fooled. Peers do approximately the same work we do and they can help us by teaching us better ways to do our work; they provide moral support; and they even stand in for us sometimes. Conversely, peers can hurt us by refusing to help, or by actively undermining our performance. It all depends on the relationships we develop.

People develop relationships based on love or hate, trust or fear, and race, gender, tradition, and other criteria. People will continue to develop relationships in these ways but what I suggest you consider, as you build relationships during this consolidation phase, is making social contracts. This means having agreements, and keeping them unless you mutually agree to change them.

Social contracts require communicating with those with whom you want relationships. They require that you express what you want from the relationship and that you listen to what the other person wants. The social contract is then negotiated between the two of you, however informally, and trust is built as the contract is honored. The social contract may cover everything from cooperative projects at work to meetings after hours. Clear social contracts will make you more effective at work, and will make work more satisfying for you.

The observant reader will notice that the themes underlying social contracts—communication, trust, relationship—are threads which weave throughout this book. This is intentional. You find them here, and you find them in life, holding together the essential fabric of our existence.

"Learn to manage yourself before you try to manage others," I was told early in my first career, and I realize now that this was sound advice. Once we learn to manage ourselves, and this includes managing our relationships with peers, we are ready for supervisory responsibility for others in our organization. We can become a boss.

Managing subordinates is a lot like managing relationships with peers. In fact, some of the most skillful bosses treat their subordinates like peers—without abdicating the direction-giving and decision-making responsibilities that are part of a boss's job. In working with subordinates, as in working with peers, I suggest creating social contracts. Some bosses demand respect, some rule by fear, others try to be liked. For lasting relationships, you need to learn the process of expressing mutual wishes and then negotiating agreements that meet the needs of those involved as well as the needs of the organization.

Managing your boss is one of the most important—and most neglected—elements of success at work. Chris Hegarty, in his book *How to Manage Your Boss*, writes that many business managers who are skillful in other parts of their job perform poorly in relating to their boss. What I recommend, and this is essentially Hegarty's advice also, is that you develop a social contract with your boss similar to those you create with others in your work environment.

Agreements with your boss cover much of the same territory as your other agreements, and some that is new. Because your boss has management responsibility, you know that he or she needs information to use in planning, organizing, leading, and controlling. Your agreement should include providing such information and, if you want a strong relationship, you will base your communications on an evolving understanding of what your boss really needs. Because your boss has the additional power that comes with the position, there may be some areas not open to negotiation, but the principle is the same and successful bosses recognize the value of input from you.

Agreements with the boss which are usually unique to that relationship cover such issues as task assignment, work location, hours worked, and vacation time. These can be crucial to job happiness, as you know by now, and you gain more control in these areas as you build your relationship with your boss.

All bosses, even if they own the business, have some limitations on what they can negotiate on central work issues. Your task is to find out how much flexibility there is, express your desires and listen to the boss's needs, and then work out agreements which reflect the evolving situation.

Sometimes the most critical agreement with the boss concerns compensation, a topic which comes under the larger heading of managing money.

Managing Money

In a recent newspaper column addressed primarily to women, Nikki Scott wrote:

> You can talk about your fears, hopes, sorrows, and victories with your closest woman friend. You can discuss marriage, children, your past and future and, occasionally, even your sex life.

> What you probably do not discuss is your salary. It's a male tradition, this secrecy about one's earning power—which isn't surprising.

Scott goes on to say that this secrecy isn't surprising because "men have been judged by how much they earn." In a culture where material possessions are exalted, it is little wonder that money—how much we have, how much we earn—is an emotionally loaded issue. As such, it is a highly charged topic in discussions with a boss.

How do you handle compensation discussions?

First of all, you need to know what others are paid for work comparable to that which you are doing. The best way to gain this knowledge is to ask directly. "If you trust a few people with information about your income, chances are a few will trust you," says Nikki Scott, and salary information in your own organization is the most valuable. People in your support network are often willing to give you salary information, too. Another excellent source is the research meetings described in Chapter Five.

If direct sources don't satisfy you, you can often find out about what others earn by reading newspaper stories about salary negotiations, or you can look in the want ads in the same paper and find out what is being offered. Want more? Look in a recent book, *The American Almanac of Jobs and Salaries*, written by John Wright, who says, "If you know what your boss knows, then you are on a more equal footing for what is essentially a confrontation situation."

Once you have salary knowledge, be sure you understand the timing involved. Some firms give raises annually, some semi-annually. Some give raises with new assignments, others wait. Some hold fast to these rules, and some allow bosses to give raises and bonuses when they see fit.

Once you understand the timing on compensation in your work environment, get a sense of how you are being evaluated. Your agreement with your boss should include the work you are expected to do, both quality and quantity, and the means of evaluation. Make sure you understand the agreement and then, if your performance is good, talk with your boss about compensation.

While such discussions are rarely easy, for *either* person, your job performance is usually the best place to start. After all, you came here to use your skills to solve problems. If you are doing this successfully, it is valuable for you and your boss to agree on that. Since problems solved mean money ahead in most organizations, this kind of discussion is a good preamble to communicating about compensation.

Success in discussions about money has as much to do with our attitude as with the amounts involved. Some people never have enough, no matter how much is flowing in. And others always seem to have enough, even with an income well below the national average. So when you consider how well you have done in a negotiation about salary, figure in your feelings about money.

A career changer by the name of Michael Phillips, who was an innovative vice president for a major bank before becoming an author and small business consultant, taught me a lot about money in his book *The Seven Laws of Money*. Several of Phillips' laws apply here.

The first law is: "Do it! Money will come when you are doing the right thing." Act, and you will find the money you need. If there is not enough money, you can ask yourself if you are doing the right thing *and* you can ask if you have correctly defined "enough money."

Another law: "Money is a dream." Money represents many of our fantasies, and the accumulation of money can make these dreams come true. Without enough money, we cannot have the home we want, the car, the travel. In Upton Sinclair's inflammatory 1906 novel *The Jungle*, Jurgis Rudkus loses his tenement "dream" house and is reduced to begging for pennies after being injured at work and losing his income. We all have legitimate, basic money needs which can be met in the work we do if we use our skills fully.

This leads to the next law: "Money is a nightmare." For Jurgis Rudkus, money became a nightmare. For the majority of those in this country's jails and prisons, money pursued for liberation has diminished freedom. Money is also a nightmare for those who fear poverty, for those who fight over money in marriages, and for those who quarrel over inheritances.

166

The final law on Phillips' list, and the final law that applies here, is: "There are worlds without money." Beyond the dreams and the nightmares of money is the reality of the human experience that transcends the need for what money buys. The joy of life is ultimately independent of money, and the joy of work does not really happen at the money level.

Managing work and managing money, as you may be sensing, finally depend on understanding our own true nature and on managing ourselves.

Managing Our Humanness

"We are all more human than otherwise," said the psychiatrist Harry Stack Sullivan. The acceptance of this truth is the start of wisdom.

Traditional business analysis is based on an assessment of organizational strengths and vulnerabilities, and this approach makes sense for individuals. What are your strengths? What skills, interests, and experiences do you have that make you distinctive from those around you? Where do you excel?

You considered such questions during the exploration stage but now, half way around the cycle in the consolidation stage, you have more data on which to base your assessment. The strengths you thought were going to be important may not be utilized much in your new work. Is this a problem for you? Conversely, you have probably discovered new strengths, or at least found some known assets to be more important than you had anticipated. Are there strengths you want to develop further? What specific steps might you take to do this?

Vulnerabilities are less pleasant to think about than strengths, yet we all have them, and understanding them gives us power. Part of the discontent that got us started on this whole journey may have stemmed from our vulnerabilities. We might have been a structured person unhappy in an unstructured organization (vulnerability: I do not function well without specific job structure). Or we might have been a creative person in a dry, staid firm (vulnerability: I do not function well when my creativity is stifled and unappreciated). As with strengths, notice which vulnerabilities have been accommodated in your new work and which have not. Which vulnerabilities no longer cause you problems? (The person who makes errors with numbers may not find that a handicap painting portraits.) Which vulnerabilities linger? (The person who antagonized bosses may continue to do so.)

In understanding both your strengths and vulnerabilities, consider first what you know to be true. Listen to that inner voice which does not lie. Learn to trust that voice. Then notice what other people tell you. Some outside feedback can be very helpful and some can give us data we had missed altogether ("Your fly is open!"). Some comments from others reflect problems they are dealing with more than any strength or vulnerability we may have. There is no easy way to know the difference, and criticism, accurate or not, can be acutely painful. The evolved people I see have come to rely more and more on their own inner voices. We should strive, I think, to do likewise.

If we are becoming more alert as we move around the careercycle, we find ourselves doing work that makes better and better use of our strengths and in which our vulnerabilities diminish in importance. Maximize your strengths; minimize your vulnerabilities. In my management career, a love of talking was sometimes a problem, especially when I was saying the wrong thing to the wrong person at the wrong time. As a teacher, however, I am paid to talk and I find the classroom a more tolerant atmosphere for ranging over the wide spectrum of topics that interest me. My propensity to gab became a more significant strength and a less serious vulnerability in a new environment.

As the song says, "Accentuate the positive."

Progress around the careercycle is not all at the same pace and the slow points have their value. During the consolidation phase, we may pause to integrate the change that has gone before and contemplate the decisions that lie ahead. If we are fortunate, we arrive at "the still point of the turning world" and see our life with new eyes.

What we see in this quiet time may well become valuable new insights for our renewed journey.

Re-Exploration

Eliot wrote that "the end of all our exploring will be to arrive where we started." The circular path arrives where it began through the critical function of exploration—continual seeking, continual inquiring—a process we began in earnest half way round the cycle from where we are now. So now we begin again to explore.

Like the seasoned explorer of uncharted lands, we may seek different answers this second time. We may investigate different terrain. We may recruit different helpers. We come this time with the new perspective of one who has successfully traversed the changepoint.

As we focus our attention once again on exploring, it is worth evaluating our approach to the task. There are three basic modes for exploring:

- *Passive*, where we start with low expectations and hope that the other person will initiate. The passive explorer would say, "You don't happen to know about . . ." and then slink away.

- *Assertive*, where we expect cooperation and express ourselves directly and clearly, taking initiative. The assertive explorer says, "I would like to know more about . . ." and, "Could you tell me . . ." and "Who should I see . . ." The assertive explorer can take "no" for an answer and is willing to ask again (and again) in a different, non-hostile, non-threatening way.

- *Aggressive*, where we expect instant service and attack the other with harsh, angry words. The aggressive explorer would say, "I've got EEO behind me, if you don't give me what I want . . ." or "I deserve . . ." and "I demand . . ." The aggressive explorer communicates anger and frustration with his body language and usually doesn't get what he came for.

The assertive explorer communicates directly and listens well, adapting according to messages received. The assertive explorer builds relationships, expanding the support network all travelers need. And the assertive explorer slips up once in a while, becoming a little passive or a little aggressive when aiming for the middle path.

Incidentally, should you want more information, an excellent book to read is *Self-Assertion for Women*, by Pam Butler.

The 80/20 rule says that eighty percent of the work is done by twenty percent of the workers, eighty percent of good ideas come from twenty percent of the philosophers, etc. Most of the people in this world are passive, at least eighty percent, and a minority creates activity. If you choose to be active, you have a terrific advantage. If you choose to be part of the twenty percent who are assertive, you have the potential to become an outstanding explorer.

Re-exploration, like the exploration we started half a cycle ago, starts with a look inward. If you saved your worksheets from the earlier period, go back now and look at your words and pictures and see what changes you notice. You probably do not need to repeat most of the exercises you did, but you *can* use the wisdom you gained coming through the changepoint to view your inner world with new eyes. Stay in touch with yourself at this level. Keep exploring.

The outer world calls for a different approach. You are now doing new work, as a result of your earlier success in exploration, and you do not need to launch a major expedition. But you can stay alert to new data in the newspapers, in books, in talks with friends, co-workers, clients, and competitors. Inquisitiveness is a habit worth keeping. Continue to be a skillful explorer and enjoy the pleasures of ongoing learning.

Consolidation is a period when we sometimes think, often not for the first time, about the possibility of going into business for ourselves. There are rich rewards and serious hazards awaiting those who actually pursue this course. There are also ways to explore the entrepreneurial path without fully committing. You can talk with people who are on their own. You can visit the place where they do business. When you find an opportunity you want to pursue further, you can often do this without giving up your present work. Direct mail businesses can be tried part-time, and so can some direct sales businesses. Most free lance work is done part-time; so is much consulting. If you think you like it, try it out—explore! —and see what you discover.

One of the best books for those who want to be on their own is *Earning Money Without a Job* by Jay Levinson. Jam-packed with good ideas, this book also offers a practical warning to what Jay calls "the economics of freedom:"

> For many people, it is definitely a poor choice. These people do not or cannot have the discipline necessary for success in a life of freedom. Many of these people have the discipline, but do not have the thick skin and determination required. Others are just too separated from reality. But most people for whom the economics of freedom is contraindicated are those who enjoy receiving orders from others, who enjoy having their work assigned to them, who enjoy the security of a regular paycheck, the assertiveness of a hardheaded boss.

Most entrepreneurs I know have a strong need to achieve, stronger than their need for power or for relationship. They take risks when they have to, yet they approach such decisions realistically. If this is you, perhaps you should consider a business of your own.

Whether a small business is right for you or not, do the exploring you need to, both inner and outer, until you are satisfied with what you find. Because sooner or later, most of us will change careers, and the skillful explorer is the one most likely to find fulfillment.

Your Next Career

"The day you start your new job is the day you start planning your next career," someone told me several years ago. I wish I could remember who, because I would like to thank that person for the sound advice. It worked for me, as you will read in Chapter Twelve, and it can work for you.

If you have read this far, you probably see some validity in the idea that work moves in cycles—in your life and in the lives of others. Some of us will go through only minor work changes, finding our present responsibilities fulfilling and never again feeling enough discontent to initiate major change. But for almost all of us, change is a possibility and it is important to be prepared. Besides, the process of preparing, the exploration, is a source of stimulation and joy in itself.

Have you been persuaded to at least start thinking about your next career?

If not, ponder the example of this career changer:

I got my engineering degree from Stanford and then found that I liked engineering but not the people doing it. These are dull twerps, I thought. This is BS.

So I went to Purdue and got an MBA and went with a large aerospace firm as a financial analyst (change #1). I became interested in computers there and got a job teaching computer science nights, figuring "if you can't do it, teach it."

The head of the computer department in my company found out about my teaching job and I went to work for him (change #2). He sent me to all the computer schools run by big computer companies, but I was already looking for another transition.

What I wanted was an opportunity to do computer consulting as a way to eventually broaden into full-time consulting. I gotta use a spring board, I figured. After a year and a half I knew all about consulting, and went to another company (change #3). I left computers behind.

In summing up this part of his career for me, this forty-two-year-old said, "When I was stalled, I switched. I used outside activities to do it." Using different words to describe a similar process, a senior executive said that he had changed careers when he "had run out of elation." Whether we change often or only once in a lifetime, whether we make dramatic changes or subtle ones, we profit by preparing ourselves.

Consolidation starts when we come back to the real world following renewal. The heart of consolidation involves using our new perspective to assess where we are. As we move out of the consolidation phase we begin to think of new work options and prepare ourselves for recommitment, the next major phase in the journey.

10

RECOMMITMENT

He has half the deed done,
Who has made a beginning.

HORACE

There is a tide in the affairs of men
which, when taken on the flood leads on to
fortune; omitted, all the voyage of their
life is bound in shallows and in
miseries; and we must take the current
when it serves or lose our ventures.

WILLIAM SHAKESPEARE

"'I realize you're never going to be happy unless you're doing things you think are worthwhile,' my wife said to me the other day." This is the seventy-year-old executive who has had leadership roles in each of his several careers. "I was touched . . . because she's right!"

This man will soon become chairman of the executive committee of his company and will continue to serve on the boards of five other major corporations. He has also committed to serve on the Executive Service Board. "You don't get paid for that," he told me. "Well, you do, but not in money."

"I want to keep my attention on the problems of others, not on my own," this leader told me. "My goal is not to get repotted in the *next* ten years." Good luck! This career changer has recommitted. He knows his goals and he knows how he wants to achieve them. For him, "not to get repotted" probably means that he does not want to go through another of the major transitions that have been the hallmark of his adult life. But for all of us, regardless of our work history, change is inevitable and recommitment is an integral part of that change.

Recommitment is the sixth and final phase in the career-cycle that began so long ago, with discontent. From this new point of view we see the cycle more clearly and we face the possibility of going around again, aware and alert. We set our goals with a new level of honesty and we lay our plans with a degree of realism that reflects the experience we have gained in our travels. We face risks with courage, sensitive to the joy inherent in the process. We know that, as we do all this, we are not alone.

Recommitment starts with setting goals.

Setting Goals

I. F. Stone, the iconoclastic Washington, D.C., writer, says:

> If you expect to see the final results of your work you have
> not asked a big enough question.

This book is about person power—finding ways to use all that we have, to be the best that we can be. The crucial point is not whether we want to be a welder, or soldier, or manager, or political activist. The crucial point is that we set our sights on becoming the best that we have in us to become.

Part of goal setting is deciding in which areas we want to have goals. Work is an obvious one. Another might have to do with our body, to lose weight or swim across the lake. Or we might have goals in our spiritual life: A friend of mine who grew up in the Pentecostal tradition has decided to become a Catholic and is now in the process of converting.

In setting goals, two important areas are learning and play, both pieces of our lives intimately interconnected with work. Consider these in terms of your life planning:

- *Learning* includes earning diplomas from degree-awarding institutions. Most readers of this book have high school diplomas and many are college graduates, yet for a lot of you, including re-entry women, earning another degree is an important goal. This is fine (I earned a Ph.D. when I was forty-four), but as I said earlier, beware of using the pursuit of a degree—comfortable work for most of us—as a way to avoid getting on with the real work in your life. Very few jobs require getting an advanced degree, even some which say that they do.

  In case you haven't noticed, learning is a consistent theme around the careercycle, and those who succeed most are those who learn best. Research meetings are perhaps the most clear-cut example, but *all* work-related activities have a lot to teach us.

  Finally, there are semi-formal ways to keep on learning. Want to become a consultant? Go to a workshop for consultants (I did). Want to become a dancer? Take lessons. Want to read faster? Take a speed reading course (I took two). So what would you like to learn about? And what are you doing about it?

- *Play* is the part of life we often denigrate, being well-trained products of the Protestant work ethic. Most of us figure that play is something called retirement that comes at the end of life as a reward for years of drudgery. The idea of the golden mean, with a sound mind in a sound body, is as relevant today as it was in ancient Greece. So plan for some fun.

  And don't be too rigid about it, like the sixty-eight-year-old executive who told me that two years earlier he had vowed to re-read the world's one hundred greatest classics. He explained how hard it was proving to be, and how he wished he hadn't set that goal, but he was going to do it if it killed him. Relax. Don't be afraid to change goals and commitments. After all, that's what learning is all about, isn't it?

Goal setting is the heart of planning. If sufficient thought and exploration have gone into creating goals, the goals will be right and the steps for achieving them will become clear. In fact, most of Chapters Four, Five, Six, and Seven are about ways to achieve goals at work.

The Question Man asked a housing management specialist, "What's your latest private improvement?" The answer:

> Putting my work in proper perspective. I was working every weekend, but now I'm concentrating on improving other parts of my life rather than my career. I admire well-rounded people.

This man has a goal. How about you? If you still want help on setting goals, pick up John Gardner's inspiring little book *Excellence*. You already know somewhere inside just where you want to go. The issue now is to get there. And get on with creating the best possible life you can have.

Creating Options

Decision makers need options. Without options, there is no decision, a condition that applies to individuals as well as organizations. Because we want to make the best possible decisions about our lives, we need to create options.

Options are action alternatives; options are real and usable choices. The depression that washes over some of us at the discontent stage often stems from a sense of having no options. We feel hopeless and impotent. The way out, for most of us, is to identify some of the many options we all have. Way back around the circle at discontent, the barriers to moving ahead seemed formidable. Here at the point of recommitment, having successfully traversed the changepoint, the barriers seem more manageable. *Now* is the time to create options.

Buried in "The Mary Gloster," a long, rambling poem by Rudyard Kipling, is a wonderful quatrain. A dying entrepreneur is telling his wastrel son about how he surpassed his competitors by launching the first steam-powered cargo vessels to ply the English Channel:

They copied all they could follow,
But they couldn't copy my mind.
And I left 'em sweating and stealing
A year and a half behind.

Creating options is how we make our lives significant. However you may feel about competition, beware of being left "a year and a half behind."

The first place to create options is in the work you are doing right now. Seek out new (or alternative) tasks that will let you develop new or unused skills. Your thinking on your long-term goals will give you a sense of direction. Perhaps you want to travel more. This is possible in many organizations. Want to develop your leadership skills? Most organizations are crying out for leaders. Want to create a new service? Most organizations are desperate for people who take initiative. Be assertive and you will see all kinds of chances to create options in your present work.

Reaching out beyond the place you are working now, you can create options among those doing similar work. The people you met during research meetings and job interviews are valuable contacts. Many of them you will want to stay in touch with and—who knows?—one of them may ask you one day about working for them, giving you another option. An executive I know interviewed with his present employer two years before he was offered a job. He and the employer both worked at maintaining contact during those two years and the result was a new agreement that satisfied both of them.

Some people create options for self-employment, or at least supplemental income. *Entrepreneur*, "The Business Opportunity Magazine," is full of ideas, and so is *Salesman's Opportunity* magazine. If your long-term plan points in this direction, try out something on your own. You stand to learn a lot and may make some money in the process.

A final category for creating options is in work not done for money. Volunteers sustain this nation. We are all helped by those who work without pay as teacher's aids, library helpers, counselors on human issues of all kinds, small business consultants, board members for non-profit organizations, and many, many others. Because we have been given to, most of us find ways to give back. There is no reason not to be assertive in this area, too, and create options for service which are consistent with our long term goals.

Creating options is something a neighbor has a knack for. He started out as an Episcopal priest in the '50s and came to California under the tumultuous reign of Bishop Pike in the '60s. Caught twice in political crossfires, he was unemployed for six months and then, capitalizing on his affinity for matters financial, he started selling life insurance. Having created this option for himself, he created others and moved over a period of several years into financial planning (after getting the necessary formal training). Today he is still creating options, ferreting out new financial products to better serve his clients.

In creating options, my neighbor took risks as, eventually, we all must if we wish to be fully human.

Taking Risks

In "The Road Not Taken," Robert Frost wrote:

> *Two roads diverged in a wood, and I—*
> *I took the one less traveled by,*
> *And that has made all the difference.*

When we follow our own inner voices we sometimes end up on a road "less traveled by." We face possible condemnation by those who know us; we face the possibility that we made the wrong decision (though I am coming to think that there are few wrong decisions in the long haul, only some that look bad at the moment). When we risk, we expose ourselves to uncertain outcomes. We all have some fear of risk—or we wouldn't be alive—and yet we all know the joy of succeeding, and the feeling in the moment of risk of having all our personal resources mobilized.

Walking by the ocean the other day, I met an "old-timer" traveling the country in his small van. He told me this story:

> When I was a kid I had a job in a factory in Milwaukee dipping tables in a coating so they could be used in chemistry labs. It was hard work and I remember I was paid seventeen cents an hour.
>
> After I had been there a few weeks I discovered that the guy next to me was making twenty cents. So I went to the boss and asked for a raise. "So you want a raise?" he said. "OK. Next week you go up to finishing on the fourth floor."
>
> When I got my next paycheck, I saw that I was still getting seventeen cents. The only raise I got was up to the fourth floor.
>
> So I quit. All my friends told me if I quit I'd end up in the state prison, but I did it anyway. I never went to prison, and after all these years I still take care of myself pretty good.

Can you see the risk this fellow took? In his eyes, it paid off.

We run risks in this life, whatever we do. *We* have a choice: we can let risks happen to us, or we can consciously seek out risks which move us toward our long-term goals. Risks can be seen in four categories, shown in Figure 11 in matrix form with examples from work.

The careercycle passes through the realm of risk starting somewhere in the discontent stage. As we become discontent, we sometimes take risks we are not aware of, unconscious

FIGURE 11

	RISK	
	Passive	Active
Unconscious	Sit and pout	Thumb nose at boss
Conscious	Come to work late	Explore work options

risks. In the exploration phase risks become more conscious, as we face new challenges. Commitment prepares us for the soul-shaking risks of the changepoint, and renewal energizes us for the risks involved in doing new work. Throughout the process we encounter risk; I encourage you to be alert to unconscious and passive risks, and to seek out those conscious, active risks that will make life better for you and for those around you.

Risks challenge different parts of our being. There are physical risks taken by skiers and mountain climbers and sometimes by those of us who have to cross city streets. There are emotional risks, the most important of which we take when we ask for what we want, knowing that we may get turned down and end up with a bruised ego (and because we know that sooner or later there is a *yes* awaiting us, we take these risks, right?). Mental risks are a lot like emotional risks. These are risks like exposing our minds to new knowledge, and facing the possibility that we may not understand (the mind is like a parachute—it doesn't work unless it's open). Finally, there are spiritual risks. What is the meaning of it all? What am I willing to risk to find out?

Several years ago I heard a story about a young loan officer in a San Diego bank who developed an ingenious scheme to loan himself money (under fictitious names) to support his penchant for gambling on horse races. When he traveled, this manager had a friend pay the loan installments, but one time the friend forgot and the bank tried to reach the borrower and the whole scheme came tumbling down. After two years in Terminal Island, a Los Angeles prison, this young man spent another year trying, with absolutely no success, to get a job. Figuring he had nothing to lose, he ran the following ad in the *Wall Street Journal*:

CONVICTED EMBEZZLER
Seeks Financial Management Position
Call 555-2112

He had more than forty responses and was working again two weeks later. See what taking a risk can do?

If you are still not convinced of the value of taking conscious risks to help achieve your long term goals, ponder these words from a recent column by Sylvia Porter:

> Your unhappiness about your job has now reached alarming peaks, with the Bureau of Labor Statistics reporting that as many as twenty-four million Americans—a full quarter of our work force—are dissatisfied with their work.
>
> The cost to employers runs into billions of dollars a year in absenteeism, reduced output, poor workmanship. The cost to our nation is incalculable, for this attitude is deeply eroding our ability to compete successfully in the world market.

Each of us needs to actively seek ways out of our unhappiness. Taking risks is part of that journey.

Up, Up, and Around?

The basic map described in this book is circular in shape. It is two-dimensional, with discontent, exploration, and commitment on the down side, and renewal, consolidation, and recommitment on the way back up. This circular map is presented partly as an antidote for the traditional maps (presented in Chapter One) which suggest that the only way to go in work is up. Yet there is a legitimate and basic human impulse to rise, an impulse that can be incorporated in the careercycle by adding a third dimension. The result is a helix, seen in Figure 12.

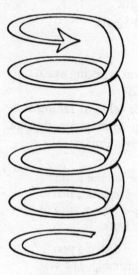

FIGURE 12

On this map, we go round and round and at the same time we have the potential of going up (or down). I first learned about this kind of map in *Radical Man* by Charles Hampden-Turner. Charles used a double helix to illustrate the idea that when others around us rise to higher levels of consciousness and behavior, we can rise, too. The helix here could represent ascending consciousness, if that is what you are interested in, or it could represent earning more and more money, if you prefer that. My sense about this third dimension is that it represents our approaching closer and closer to the very best that we can be. If we are blessed, we move in that direction all our lives.

Superman cries out "Up, up, and away" as he soars off to stupendous feats. Let us cry "Up, up and around" as we commit to developing the unlimited potential within us.

Join the Club

When the Question Man asked, "What's your latest private improvement?" a banking analyst responded:

> Going back to school. Banking is not for me. I want to do something where I can express myself. I'm studying painting and ideally I'll use it for commercial art or teaching painting.

This young woman has committed to change. Have you?

Imagine that there is a club of people committed to making their work life better. There are lots of members and there is no discrimination because of age, race, religion, income, or the number of mistakes you have made in the past. Those in the club welcome new members with open arms. Your dues are already paid, many times over. You are the membership committee. You decide if you want in. All you need to do is commit to going around again, consciously.

Because when you come to the top of the careercycle you have recommitted and, one way or another, you will be making the journey again.

11

PAUSE AT
THE TOP

Going on means going far.
Going far means returning.

TAO TE CHING

Every calling is great when greatly pursued.

OLIVER WENDELL HOLMES

"Home, in one form or another, is the great object of life," wrote Josiah Holland. The form that *home* takes in the careercycle is the pause at the top, the period that comes after recommitment and before moving again into discontent and change. Figure 13 shows us where we are.

Because we better understand what we have been through, the discontent that lies ahead now creates less anxiety. In fact, when we recognize what lies beyond discontent, this next phase becomes almost an old friend, an ally who leads us to change and then to renewal and more. From our perch at the top we see more than ever before and we know that "going on means going far."

The top of the cycle is the home point in the Hero's Journey and it has this meaning in the careercycle, too. This is the place to pause, feeling safe, before moving on again. From this vantage point we may review our progress, and the mistakes and the successes that made this progress possible. This perspective allows us to consider our future and our options in a new light.

FIGURE 13

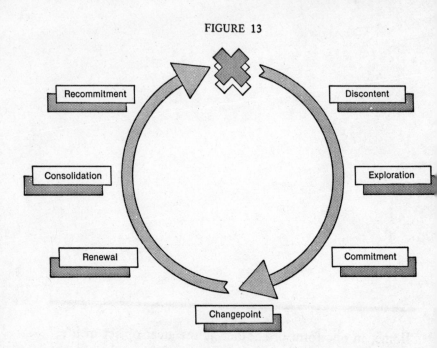

Pain in Work

The president of a world-famous research and consulting company told me this story:

> In World War II I was in the Army and had a Japanese-American outfit under my command. As punishment for breaking weekend curfew, the men had to run up to nine miles Monday morning.

> There was this one Hawaiian fellow who had to do the maximum distance *every* Monday. And every time he finished that run with the biggest smile on his face you ever saw.

> I only hope that when I finish up this run called life, I can be wearing a smile like that.

There is pain in life and there is pain in work. Usually, like the Hawaiian soldier, we create our own pain. No matter where we put the responsibility, it is crucial not to forget the joy available to us beyond the pain.

As we contemplate the journey ahead, we know that pain awaits us. It may be mostly out of our control, like this experience described in a newspaper column by a Birmingham woman:

> "He came to the door, and I thought he'd been mugged or had a car wreck; his face was gray," she said of her then husband.
>
> "His boss had called him in and said the company had been sold. When he finished his current sales projects, my husband's services would no longer be needed."

The end result? Their communication dried up, their "sex life came to a halt," and their marriage ended in divorce. Terrific pain! For some of us, it takes this much pressure to get us moving into exploration and around the cycle. For those of you reading these words, movement can be easier.

Pain at work takes many forms. Each of us has a sense of our particular form and intensity of pain. Many words were written about pain in the chapter on discontent, but one particular form of pain becomes especially clear after a trip around the careercycle. This is the condition known as "burnout."

Burnout is when "jobs that used to mean so much, have become drudgery with no associated feeling of reward," writes Dr. Herbert Freudenberger. The fire that burned brightly in us at the beginning has diminished to a flicker and threatens to go out. Like other pain and discontent, we can respond to burnout by re-examining our goals and exploring options—both within and outside of our current employment. Like other pain and discontent, the onset of burnout is a signal to begin considering change, to begin seeking the joy hiding on the other side of our problem.

Joy in Work

A brilliant academic came to see me for advice several years ago. A gifted teacher and scholar with a Ph.D. in the Liberal Arts, she was "burned out" on teaching and had taken the Civil Service exam in order to become a letter carrier for the U. S. Postal Service. She figured, logically enough, that she needed a total change in her work life with free time in the evenings to pursue her scholarly interests.

Fortunately for this young woman and for the many she serves, the Post Office turned her down. Within days, she accepted a senior administrative post in an academic institution where almost all of her many skills are put to use. She serves with distinction, and one has only to see her in action to know that she finds joy in her work.

Like this outstanding leader, each of us can emerge from burnout or our own form of discontent and find joy in work. Like this woman, a large part of our success springs from having a goal larger than ourselves.

Viktor Frankl, the psychiatrist, author, and professor who survived Auschwitz, has taught us a great deal about man's search for meaning. In a short movie I saw several years ago, Frankl drew on the chalkboard a diagram that illustrated his thinking on meaning (Figure 14).

Pursuing a meaningful goal produces happiness (it ensues), says Frankl, but if we pursue happiness directly, we are unlikely to get what we seek. This pause at the top of the cycle is a time to reconsider our goals, and to notice how we pursue meaning in our lives. It is as natural as breathing for us to do so, and our success in seeking out meaning for our existence determines the happiness we find.

194

FIGURE 14

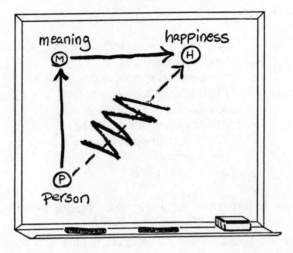

If you want an example for inspiration, consider Benjamin Franklin. This eighteenth-century Philadelphian published *Poor Richard's Almanack*, helped establish the University of Pennsylvania, and proved the identity of electricity by flying his kite in a thunderstorm. He went on to serve as deputy post master general of the Colonies and to help draft the Declaration of Independence, which he signed. He was a successful diplomatic agent to France for the new republic, and instrumental in negotiating the peace with England. In his many careers, Franklin was consistently aiming for something larger than himself.

Balance

Pain in life is balanced by joy in life, just as pain in work is balanced by joy in work. We cannot have all of one and none of the other, any more than we can eat continually or sleep continually. Balance is the law of nature, the law of life.

"Fire and Ice" by Robert Frost beautifully illustrates balance:

> Some say the world will end in fire
> Some say in ice.
> From what I've tasted of desire
> I hold with those who favor fire.
> But if it had to perish twice,
> I think I know enough of hate
> To say that for destruction ice
> Is also great
> And would suffice.

Balance is important in work, also. Notice how the career-cycle is balanced in Figure 15.

Each phase in the careercycle is balanced by the phase opposite, just as a wheel that turns without vibration is balanced one side against the other.

FIGURE 15

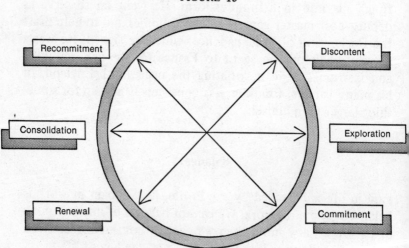

- Discontent is balanced with Renewal. The intensity of our discontent will be matched very closely with the intensity of our sense of renewal. The depth of our despair at the discontent phase is equalled by the height of our exuberance in the renewal phase. Like the newly released prisoner, our joy in being free reflects the horror of being caged.

- Exploration is balanced with Consolidation. The depth and intensity of our inner and outer exploration is matched by the breadth of our consolidation. The more we have explored, the more we have uncovered, the further we have gone, the broader the range of what we have to pull together half a cycle later. Like a gold miner who has worked long and hard, we know we will be dealing with diverse riches in a time ahead.

- Commitment is balanced by Recommitment. The intensity of the first is matched by the intensity of the second. The scope of the first—how big a change did we commit to?—is reflected in the scope of the second. We learn the power of commitment the first time through and then, half way round the cycle, recommitment is less awesome. Though our recommitment is more to the career-cycle process than to a specific change, its intensity may be even greater than our initial commitment because of the self-confidence we have accumulated.

Just as the three pairs of phases must be in balance, all six must be roughly equal for the full process to be in balance. This is built into the careercycle map because the intensity of our discontent dictates the depth of our exploration, which in turn influences the power of our commitment. If all three of these first are intense, then the next three—renewal, consolidation, and recommitment—are likely to be intense also. If the three first phases are mild—if they deal with only a portion of our work life, for example—then the three phases that follow will be mild also.

In fact, one way to view cycles of varying intensity is to see them as cycles within cycles. As argued earlier, the circular map merely reifies the twenty-four hour light/dark cycle, the twenty-eight day full moon cycle, the 365 day summer/winter cycle, and others found in nature. These cycles within cycles found in nature might translate into the careercycle map like that shown in Figure 16.

FIGURE 16

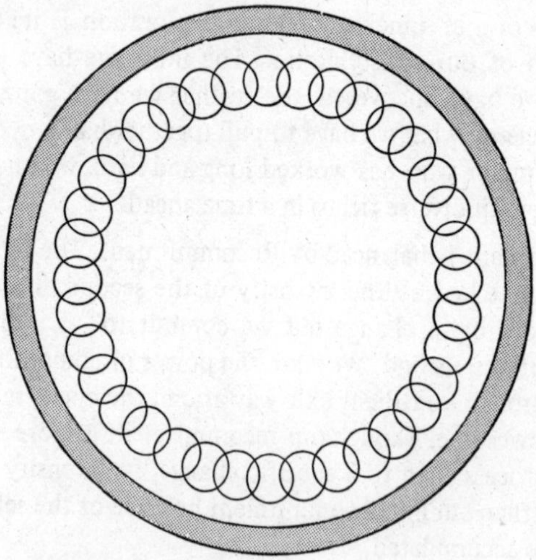

Each mini-cycle contains the same six phases found in the larger careercycle. We may not notice some of them, but they happen nonetheless. If we understand that this is happening, we can go forward with more confidence and alertness.

A middle-aged man in a recent workshop has spent several years making the transition from head of a public service agency to a management position in private industry. In that time he has gone through several mini-cycles: working as a carpenter, starting a house cleaning service, and running seminars within his church are three that I know of. In this workshop he talked about his future.

"Some people when they realize they are about to die

say, 'Oh, shit!' " he told us with tears in his eyes. "I am not going to be one of those. I am taking the plunge now."

The plunge, for him, is to take a part-time accounting job with a friend who is building a new business. If it works out as both expect, the man will become assistant to the president in six months, at a salary of $30,000 a year. The mini-cycles of the past three years are becoming part of the larger careercycle which seems about to take this man on to new and fulfilling work.

In another time, a comparable plunge was taken by Henry David Thoreau when he went to live by Walden Pond. Using more genteel language, Thoreau described his motivation thusly:

> I went to the woods because I wished to live deliberately,
> to front only the essential facts of life, and see if I could
> not learn what it had to teach, and not, when I came to die,
> to discover that I had not lived.

Most of us played with tops, those fascinating spinning spheres, when we were young; it still amazes me how they stand up. Many of us have sailed in ships which contained a spinning gyroscope somewhere in the hold to keep the vessel steady in heavy seas. The cycles in our worklife, like the gyroscope, offer stability in movement. Without movement the power vanishes; but with movement, and it is movement we have the energy to create, the potential for power is endless.

Old Maps, New Maps

Here are further lines from T. S. Eliot's "Little Gidding," words that offer a special perspective for our pause at the top:

What we call the beginning is often the end. And to make an end is to make a beginning. The end is where we start from.

This book started with two traditional maps—the salary graph and the pyramid—which no longer serve us as well as they might. The last ten chapters have described a new map, a circular model for understanding work in our lives. The careercycle map, like the 1529 map of the world (Figure 17), serves a purpose but is actually imprecise and primitive.

FIGURE 17

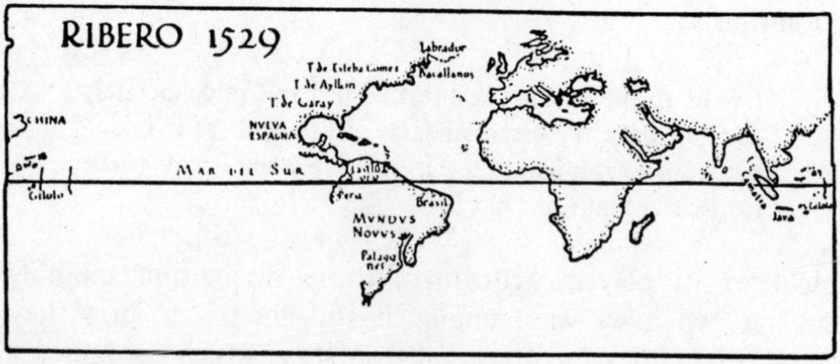

The careercycle map, like this 400-year-old world map, is at best an approximation. The map, as Gregory Bateson was fond of reminding us, is not the territory. Our own first hand experience of the territories of both the world and of work is many times richer than any map or model. Maps are a helpful starting place, but they are only useful to the extent that we understand them and make them useful.

12

**AROUND AGAIN:
ONE MAN'S
JOURNEY**

There are two kinds of people in this world,
Jack—those who live and learn
and those who just live.

JOHN A. CAPLE (1905-1979)

What counts is what you learn
after you know it all.

ETHEL BARRYMORE

"As we grow, we inspire others by being ourselves," a special teacher once told me. This friend has been an example of her own aphorism, openly shaping her career as a counselor and sharing her current struggles about which part of the country to live in and whether to go for a Ph.D.

This chapter is for those with courage and curiosity. Courage is needed if you think (as I used to) that people who write books don't make mistakes, then or now. If you want to preserve any illusion like that, you should put this book down right now. Curiosity is valuable for following the ups and downs of one man's journey. You should, like me, have a bit of the snoop in you to benefit from these last pages.

The more I work with people, the more I am in awe of the diverse ways in which we learn. Some of us learn best by lectures, some by discussions. Some of us do better listening, some doing. Some learn best with words, some with images—graphs and photos and art. Some like direct exposition, others prefer metaphors, stories, poems. Some learn best by having theory explained, others by example—by seeing theory in action. For those in that last category, this chapter is for you.

For me, the benefit of learning by example and metaphor and parable is that it is less painful. It is less direct. I can project my own life onto another and let the truth about me sink in as it will—which is usually faster than the "this is the way you should do it" approach, which stimulates my stubbornness and resistance and puts my brain in gear creating all sorts of reasons I *shouldn't* do it that way. "Why can't learning be easy?" I wonder, like Winston Churchill, who said:

> Personally, I am always ready to learn, although I do not always like being taught.

So, this chapter is not so much to teach you anything, but to offer you an opportunity to learn whatever you like and perhaps to laugh a little in the process as you consider one man's journey.

The Wellspring

John Caple was born in Toledo, Ohio in 1937, the first of four children of John A. and Frances Caple. The family would probably be described as upper middle class—comfortable, with a small business and farms for economic support. John's father worked for *his* father in the A. B. Caple Company, an alfalfa dehydrating firm, and he was president of the company when he died, fifty-two years after first going on the payroll. John's mother, in common with most women of the time, was not employed outside the home except for a stint with the American Red Cross during World War II.

John's great grandfather and namesake owned and

operated a hardware store in Alma, Michigan before retiring early and helping his son start the A. B. Caple Company (please stay tuned, the genealogy is almost over). John's grandfather on his mother's side, Charles E. Swartzbaugh, had a manufacturing plant in Toledo producing home appliances.

In terms of work, John was surrounded by the small business values of independence and economic freedom. His father often said, "I'd rather sell apples out of a cart on Cherry Street (skid row in Toledo) than be president of General Motors." And one of the most powerful family values, probably articulated by John's grandfather Caple, was "You can tell the value of a man by looking in his bankbook."

Work in John's youth taught him a lot. For example:

- a lawn mowing contract when he was fourteen taught John the value of friends: he got the job by bidding $65 (for a summer-long job involving lots of hours) when he heard from a pal that his competitor was bidding $70.
- stacking baled hay and loading one hundred pound sacks of alfalfa meal for a couple of summers showed John why he was planning to go to college: he didn't want to do *that* forever!
- putting in twelve-hour days six days a week for $100 a month on a cattle ranch in Montana the summer he was seventeen was John's first serious exploration of a possible career (cattle rancher).
- driving trucks a couple of summers showed John how much he loved power, the thrill of being in control.
- selling used cars for a local Chevrolet dealer taught John never to sell something he doesn't believe in (he *still* feels guilty about the garbage man who paid $50 for a Nash Rambler without ever learning that the left front window was missing).

Malcolm Ward, an Episcopal minister, was a guiding force in those years up to eighteen. In fact, if it hadn't been for the powerful family bias toward business, John might have gone into the ministry. What careercycles *that* decision would have put in motion!

John Whitaker, a high school coach, inspired John after an eighth grade basketball defeat, with these words of doggerel poetry (attributed to Edmund Vance Cooke):

If you think you're beaten, you are
If you think you dare not, you don't.
If you'd like to win, but you think you can't,
It's almost a cinch you won't.

If you think you'll lose, you've lost,
For out in the world you'll find
Success begins with a person's will.
It's all in the state of mind.

For many a race is lost
Ere even a step is run,
And many a coward falls,
Ere even his work's begun.

Think big and your deeds will grow;
Think small and you'll fall behind.
Think that you can and you will;
It's all in the state of mind.

If you think you're outclassed, you are;
You've got to think high to rise.
You've got to be sure of yourself
Before you can win the prize.

Life's battles don't always go
To the stronger or faster man,
And sooner or later the one who wins
Is the one who thinks he can.

These words also taught John that enthusiasm has its limits: he suggested once that his little sister read them in an all-school convocation and shared her hurt when her fellow students cried, "Corny!" There is a right place and a right time for everything, right?

Coach Whitaker once recruited John to run a leg in a mile relay with the words, "You won't have to run that hard." John cruised around and lost the race, but gained a powerful learning: no matter what *anyone* says, always do your best.

Picture a socially awkward, six-foot six-inch, 165 pounder with spectacles. That was John. By the time he was a high school senior, long hours of solitary shooting had made him a basketball "star," and his penchant for memorizing names (his mother told John that the sound people most like to hear is their own name) had propelled "friendly" John into the student body presidency. Hard work leads to power, he was discovering.

Moving Out

"Move 'em out!" bawls the trail boss, and the cattle begin to stir. At age eighteen, John moved on out, heading for Stanford University in California. His main reason for going was to play basketball, but he also learned a lot—in the classroom and out—and met Anne-Marie Lloyd, whom he later married.

John studied economics at Stanford, since this was the closest he could come to learning to be a successful businessman. He had always felt the pressure, as the oldest son, to go into the family business, so after graduating in June of 1959, he headed back to Toledo.

Looking back, this seems like a time of exploration. John found that he was more interested in adventure than in the routines he found in this little business, more interested in growth than in the stability he found. He also remembers the pain of making mistakes: he once misquoted the price for a carload of alfalfa and though the customer held him to it, he told John, "If that's the biggest business mistake you ever make, you'll be damn lucky."

Americans are voracious consumers of insurance, and John got a big piece of his by going to the Harvard Business School after fifteen months in the family business. If you want to be a success in something, he figured, get a degree in it from the best school you can find. So he went to Harvard and worked like a demon not to flunk out.

Almost two years later, with the insurance policy almost in hand, dutiful John decided to accept his father's offer and go back to the family business. A week after the decision was made, and offers declined from three major corporations, John's father called at seven one morning to say, "No, you shouldn't come back here." John, whose wife was expecting their first child in a couple of months, was slack-jawed. He called Procter & Gamble back. "So you want to eat a little humble pie?" he was asked, and responded in the affirmative.

"Reversals usually work out for the best," John will tell you, and perhaps this philosophy derives from that cold spring morning in Boston. What seemed devastating at the time, worked out beautifully career-wise, and enriched the long-term father-son relationship.

"It's like playing baseball for the Yankees," people used to say about working for Procter & Gamble. Yes, there was pride and, yes, the young men worked hard, especially in the advertising department, where John found himself. The initial burst of enthusiasm (renewal energy) carried John through a first promotion and a six month sales assignment (which he thrived on). But P&G was numbers-oriented and John was not, so he often made errors. P&G was well-organized and John was not, often making unorthodox decisions on priorities. And somehow it gnawed on John knowing that Tide cost perhaps a fifth of what it sold for and P&G had all these millions, yet the welfare mother who paid seventy-two cents for a box of detergent had to buy cat food for her children. . . .

John's boss called him in and made it clear that if John did not perform better he would not be promoted again. John was already struggling to keep up and now this. Maybe it was time to leave steamy Cincinnati. Maybe it was time to go to work for a smaller company.

So John wrote lots of letters and made lots of phone calls and before long he had five job offers (not being much of an overachiever) in San Francisco. With a brave face, John and his wife and two children headed off for the land of the golden sun.

First Time Around

When did John's first career start? With his first business dealings at age fourteen? At the A. B. Caple Company after college? At P&G? All of these were part of the foundation, but the heart of his first career was the seven years he spent with the American Potato Company (dehydrated potato products) in San Francisco.

The renewal phase lasted two years. John became the resident expert with marketing numbers because he was far more organized than his boss. He was a hero! More important, he worked with highly creative product research people to develop outstanding new products, and encountered enormous joy in the process. And he found how much he enjoyed a boss who let him run free.

A kind of consolidation occurred with the arrival of a new boss. Things became more organized and less fun. Before long discontent grew and focussed, finally, on the issue of money: "You will never make more money than you are now if you stay in marketing," John's boss told him. "You must go into sales to keep growing with this company."

Exploration was almost non-existent. Full of anger and ego energy, John said, "Hell, I'll do it." Commitment. And done at a time, John knew, that was not convenient for his boss.

The changepoint came in a meeting of the entire marketing group several days after the salary discussion when John's boss announced, "John is going to become Western Regional Sales Manager." John choked. This was news to him. This wasn't supposed to happen so fast. This meant leaving the friends in product research, moving away from the area of established successes, and striking out into unknown territory. Scary!

For the first time in his memory, John couldn't sleep the night after the announcement was made.

And yet it was less than a month before John began to feel the energy of renewal. Learning new skills, working with new people, traveling to new places—all were stimulating. The apex of renewal came in the first year when John regained the lost business of two of the largest customers in his region. New success, new joy.

Yet it wasn't long before all the travel of being a sales manager started to wear thin, both on John and on his family. And the challenges became less exciting. John took on the marketing of a new french fry program, and, despite lots of effort from everyone, it wasn't going well. After almost seven years in the potato business, John was ready for change.

Second Time Around

The second time around the careercycle was the biggie. The transition from marketing to sales, while traumatic, involved many of the same skills and took place in a single organization. The transition from management to education would involve dramatically different skills in a new and quite different type of organization. In this second transition, the stages of the careercycle develop clearly.

Discontent was brewing in the last months at the American Potato Company. Relations had deteriorated between John and his boss; when the chance came to take a job as New Business Development Manager at Dymo Industries, at a $5000 raise, John went for it.

Something bigger was cooking, though, and after nine months at Dymo, John was told to look for another job either inside or outside the company. Dymo taught John a great deal, yet somehow his heart wasn't in it. Maybe it was the Creative Initiative Foundation that John and his wife got involved with at that time, to improve their lives and change the world. Maybe John was bored. Maybe John was getting a message and not listening.

Maybe getting back into the food industry would solve John's problems. So John took a job as Director of Marketing for an Oakland food processor, with another raise in pay. Again there was the excitement of a new job, but before long John noticed that the best part of his day was the noontime run around Lake Merritt.

Then one day John went into his boss's office to see about a raise for a product manager he had hired and his boss, the executive vice president, said without preamble: "We're letting you go."

"Jesus," was all John could say, for what seemed like three minutes.

John came home that afternoon and cried, cried hard, in Anne's arms. He realized afterwards that his son, then ten years old, had witnessed that scene, and part of why this book is being written is so that his son can have a broader perspective on work.

Could the pain of discontent get any worse? As it turns

out, yes, it could. John was shaken, but he kept charging ahead, with his great background and brave face. After being unemployed for three months, a major executive search firm asked him to go visit a company in Idaho that was looking for a vice president of sales and marketing. So John and his wife were flown to Idaho, wined and dined, and John was offered the job at $40,000 a year, with a thirty-percent bonus, and lots of perks. Tempting, especially to Anne, but wasn't this just inviting more of the same pain and discontent?

Exploration finally started about then, a year or two late, when John took a job with a small food-brokerage firm for $15,000 a year. John knew that change was getting ready to happen, and though he wasn't sure what kind, he did want to try a smaller firm and a job he was more comfortable with. He also learned about his big ego, when he realized afterwards that the biggest thing that happened to him in that year and a half was when he was named a vice president, along with the other sales people. You should hear him brag!

Exploration began in earnest not long after John joined this little company. He and Anne left Creative Initiative Foundation and within a month, in September, 1975, John was teaching marketing one night a week to MBA students at Golden Gate University. He had found in Creative Initiative that he loved leading groups; teaching was a logical next step.

As 1976 opened, John found he was enjoying the one night of teaching each week far more than the five days of doing business. What is more, he was getting praise and affirmation as a teacher that he had never gotten in business. Change was getting ready to happen.

About this time John had a dream one night, which still seems pivotal. In the dream, he went into a twelve-story building to see Jerry West, the basketball star, on the eleventh floor. After seeing West, he wanted to go down, but the elevator wouldn't come. An Oriental man seemed to be guarding it. After twenty minutes of intense frustration, John figured he could take an up elevator and then go on down.

John woke in a sweat, the feeling of impotence still real in his belly. And yet the dream offered hope. Instead of blindly trying one way—going from marketing job to marketing job—perhaps he could achieve his life goals by trying a different route.

On July 1, a few days later, Anne gave him the book *Shifting Gears* as a fifteenth-wedding-anniversary gift. Written by Nena and George O'Neill, this paperback describes how change, including career change, can happen.

Then on July 14, 1976, *commitment* came, as clear as a light turning on in a dark room. John and his wife and two children had eaten dinner at the Irma Hotel in Cody, Wyoming and were driving on through the night hoping to get into Yellowstone Park by midnight. Driving their VW bus across deserted Wyoming, John and Anne talked about his teaching full-time and the lifestyle involved and finally John said, "Why not?" and Anne said, "Why not?" and the thing was done.

With commitment, exploration narrowed to college teaching opportunities. John told the owner of the brokerage firm of his plans and stayed with the firm three months longer, meanwhile using the Bolles approach to get "informational interviews" with eighteen different colleges and universities. Like the research meetings recommended here, they worked beautifully, and by the time John got into serious job negotiations, he knew more about local business administration programs than most of those he was talking with.

For John, the *changepoint* came over Labor Day weekend, 1976. A friend and his wife came to visit and the friend told John all the reasons his decision would never work financially, while the wife told him that there was no chance for a thirty-nine-year-old without a Ph.D. to make it in academia (she had a university appointment, and she knew!).

John came out of this as depressed as he had been in years. His mind filled with suicidal fantasies. "My God! What have I done?" he thought.

As he came out of the trough, he made a list of action options, things he could do (suicide was not on the list). He chose the third or fourth item, which was to see a career counselor who had led a workshop he had taken, a solid citizen named Charles Prugh. And three days later Charlie said, "You're OK; you're on the right track." And that was what John needed. He was on his way again.

"Good luck comes to those who see the customers," the old sales manager said, and about a week later John's exploring paid off when he had a phone call from someone who had heard about him from Charlie Prugh. It turned out that Dominican College, a small liberal arts institution six miles from John's home, was looking for someone to head their brand-new business administration department, and would John be interested? You can bet your bottom dollar John was interested!

Job interviews took all fall, Dominican being a conservative institution, and on Christmas Eve, 1976, John was offered chairmanship of the business department. One fantastic Christmas gift!

Three days later John accepted, and the transition to the world of education was complete.

So was John a success in his fourteen-year business career? He had lots of good ideas, hired and trained fine people, and developed new products that still make handsome profits for their owners. Or was he a failure? Lots of his ideas were duds, some of his new product failures were stupendous, and he never left a company unless he was fired or departed under a cloud. Success or failure? You decide. But whatever you conclude, notice how much John learned in those fourteen years . . . in spite of himself.

John was not out of the woods yet. He knew that academic salaries were low by business standards, but Dominican

College was low even by academic standards. John gulped and Anne gulped twice. A trusted counselor, David Jacobsen, listened to the upset over money and then told them, "If John can't earn that much again with his outside activities, I'll eat my hat." Dave's comment saved the day, and, as it turned out, there was enough money (which is why John is a believer in the first law of money: "If you are doing what's right, there will be enough money").

Renewal came in waves, and although John is still on a high from his adventure, the full flush of renewal came in the first two years in education.

John brought new ideas and new energy to the classroom, and his students responded. His classes grew in size and the business department grew and, before too many semesters had passed, it was the largest undergraduate department at the college. John hired part-time and full-time faculty members, counseled students, coordinated with the administration, and taught a course overload—all on a surge of renewal energy.

You may have registered that renewal benefits others. John's rebirth attracted people to him who wanted career counseling, it brought students who were interested in business careers, and it even induced a local school board member to ask if John would be willing to lead a career change workshop for displaced teachers (yes, of course he would).

And the latest form for this re-circulation of energy is the book you are reading now, a way John sees to reach people with what he has learned without charging them $65 an hour.

Consolidation for John overlapped with renewal and still continues. He still has boss problems and likes to tell this story:

Two men met on the road between two towns. The first asked the second, "What are the bosses like in yonder town?"

215

"What are they like in the town you just left?" he was asked.

"They are all pig-headed and ornery and won't listen to a thing."

"Well, that's the way you'll find them in the town ahead, too," he was told.

John still has trouble being organized, although organization is less important now and he is more inspired to be good at it. John still has trouble with numbers, although his life is such that this is not debilitating. John still has a short attention span—he gets bored easily (Fritz Perls said, "If you're bored, you're not paying attention").

John also saw in the consolidation phase that the strengths he identified earlier were important. He is a leader, an initiator, a communicator, a teacher. He's good at talking and pretty good at listening. His ability to work with college age people surprised him and he had not anticipated how good he would feel being part of the community that is Dominican College.

Recommitment, the sixth of the six stages on the career-cycle, happened for John the day he started work at Dominican, and continues to have an impact. As he had been advised, he decided on his next career the first day he reported for work, and that career was seminar leader. That and several other mini-careers have ripened in the days which followed:

- John had two sub-goals in exploring a future career as seminar leader: to do management training seminars for IBM and to lead seminars at Esalen Institute in Big Sur, California. He has done both (and *that* is scary: he now thinks more about what he wants, realizing that he is likely to get it). John loves leading seminars but would not want to do it full-time.

- John did some educational and management consulting, like all aggressive business professors do, and found himself lacking. He

216

is fine on the people part, but not analytical enough to do traditional consulting.

- John stumbled into career counseling and loves it. He plans to continue doing this kind of work, including outplacement counseling, and will continue leading career workshops.
- John acted on an unfilled desire from his college days to study abroad and started a "Dominican at Oxford" program at his college. John and his family went to England the summer of 1979 and he has continued to provide leadership for this successful venture. John learned that he would like teaching abroad to be part of his future.
- Finally, John is exploring the career implications of writing a book. He is learning about authors and agents and publishers and talk shows and the lecture circuit. Who knows what this will bring?

All of which does not mean that John doesn't continue to struggle. Several months ago he was turned down for promotion to associate professor (he was since been promoted) and in the upset that followed, he thought, "I'll show them, I'll go get a better teaching job at a higher rank." A few weeks later, it occurred to him to follow some of his own advice (Counselor, heal thyself!) and test out the change before plunging. So he taught one semester at San Francisco State, where he found that although he loved the teaching, the commute was a killer and parking was horrible . . . and he decided that he would rather be part of a smaller organization . . . like Dominican College.

Unfinished Chapter

"Meet with triumph and disaster," Kipling says, "and treat those two imposters just the same." The rest of the adventure for John will contain both triumph and disaster, though when and in what proportions God only knows.

Unfinished business for John includes this book. How

broadly will it be exposed? How well will it serve those who read it? How successful will it be as a springboard for the ideas that build on it? From a career standpoint, how skillful will John be in doing all that needs to be done for this book to reach its goals? What unexpected learnings lie ahead?

Unfinished business for John includes his role at Dominican College. He is hoping for a sabbatical in the not too distant future to renew his energy and explore options. He dreams of establishing a Career Development Center at Dominican College to do career counseling, workshops, and research. He dreams of expanding upon the Dominican at Oxford program. Here, too, unexpected learnings lie ahead.

For each of us, the rest of our days are an unfinished chapter, a chapter whose pages will be filled with both agony and ecstasy. For each of us, work is a central part of that chapter, and a part we may have more control over than we ever before thought possible.

Coda

In musical terminology, the coda is "a concluding passage, the function of which is to bring a composition to a proper close." Somewhat obscure, the term is nonetheless brief and precise and appropriate here.

Careercycles is a guidebook for those who work. Like any good guidebook, it offers a map to orient the traveler and tells what to expect at each point on the map. It identifies guideposts, both physical and emotional. And it provides specific directions on how to get from one point to another.

The map in *Careercycles*, like the ultimate map of planet earth, is round. The circular careercycle, like paths taught in many ancient religions, tells us that we will go through the same experiences again and again in life. Acknowledging this, we proceed on the path more alertly and find more success and fulfillment in our journey.

Careercycles is built on a simple idea but describes an enormously complex process. That complexity is touched on in this book, and is embraced most comprehensively in the vignettes and anecdotes reported here. These real-life glimpses offer the best understanding. These are the heart of a message designed to offer the reader an opportunity for greater success in the job market and a new perspective on satisfaction at work.

One of our first discoveries when we learn to ride a bicycle is that if we stop, we fall down. Work is like that. We must keep going—learning, exploring, stretching, risking. With careercycles, as with bicycles, movement is essential.

This last chapter is called "Around Again." I intend to go around again . . . and again. How about you?

As you leave this book, go with these words from Kahlil Gibran:

> *Work is love made visible.*
>
> *When you work with love*
> *you bind yourself to yourself,*
> *and to one another,*
> *and to God.*

APPENDIX A:
TOOLS FOR
EXPLORATION

These twenty tools for exploration can help you as you move around the careercycle, particularly as you approach the commitment phase. Although these tools come from many sources—Dick Bolles, Mary Harper, Tom Jackson, Natalie Rogers, and Sid Simon are some I can identify—they have all been modified based on my experience in workshops and counseling clients. These tools for exploration are grouped by category, to help you pick those that might be most useful.

Who Am I?

Tool #1. Looking back over the years, who are the three most significant people in your life? List their names and the kinds of work they did. For each, write the reasons they were significant for you. What did you particularly admire about each?

Tool #2. Write down ten things you are *not*, ten identities that do not belong to you. Beside each, write the reasons that this is not you. Then put a one beside that which is most unlike you, a two beside that which is second most unlike you, and so on, until you have ranked five non-identities.

Tool #3. Write down ten things you *are*, ten identities that you claim for yourself. Beside each, write the reason or reasons that this is you. Then put a one beside that which is most important, a two beside that which is second most important, and so on, until you have ranked the first five.

Tool #4. Think of a trusted friend or counselor, someone who knows you better than anyone, and write down ten words that person would use to describe you. Circle the most important words.

Tool #5. Make a list of those things that you value most highly (for example, "having money," "world peace," "accomplishment," "freedom," "happiness," "excitement," or "wisdom"). Think of as many values as you can. Then put a one beside that which is most important, a two beside that which is second most important, and so on, until you have ranked the first five.

Where Am I Now?

Tool #6. Turn to the next appendix (Appendix B) and take the twenty question career quiz. Use the interpretation guide to get a sense of where you are, and write a paragraph describing your understanding.

Tool #7. Write down ten skills you possess (skills are things you are able to *do*). Rank the first five in order of importance, with one as the most important, two as the second most important, and so on.

Tool #8.   Write down the skills you are using in your present work or were using in your most recent work. Circle the ones you are best at. Now draw a line under your list and add skills you possess and would like to use in your work, or use more frequently.

Tool #9.   On a plain sheet of paper, write a phrase describing the kind of work you are doing now or were doing most recently. Draw a circle around your words. Outside that circle write down parts of that job (for example, "writing reports," "selling service contracts," or "washing dishes"). Circle each of these parts with a smaller circle than the one in the center. Try to find "parts" to go all the way around the job balloon in the center. Then draw a straight line from the job balloon to the parts of the job you like, and a zigzag line to the parts of the job you do not like. If you like the part a lot, or dislike it a lot, make the line thicker. Write a paragraph at the bottom of your balloon picture about what you have learned from the exercise.

Tool #10.   Fold a large sheet of plain paper in two (vertically). Using marking pens, pastels, and crayons, and drawing with your right hand, create the right side of your body on the left margin of the paper before you. Then turn the paper over and, drawing with your left hand, create the left side of your body. Then unfold the paper and notice what you see. Are there parts of you that are not getting used? Are there parts of you that you would like to develop further? Are there strengths you see in this picture that you had not noticed before? Write a paragraph at the bottom of your picture answering these questions and giving your impressions.

What Do I Want?

Tool #11. Write a classified advertisement for the help wanted section of the newspaper describing your perfect job —the ad you would most want to see and the job you would most want to be hired for. Start with the name of the job and include details like where you would work, when you would work, who you would work with, and who your boss would be. Include a salary and starting date.

Tool #12. Write down five tasks that other people get paid for but which you would do for free, for the joy of it. Beside each write what you like about that task.

Tool #13. Write down a dollar figure that represents the amount you *need*, before taxes, to live for a year. Take your time and include the cost of food, clothing, a place to live, transportation, and any "necessary" extras. Then estimate your tax payments and get the total figure. Next, write down a dollar figure that represents the amount you would *like to have*, before taxes, to spend in a year. Make a list of what you would do differently if you had this higher amount. Finally, write down those things that keep you from getting the amount you would like to have. Pay particular attention to those things you can change.

Tool #14. Imagine that you have just received a telegram telling you that you will be getting a million dollars a year, tax free, for the rest of your life. What would you do in the first year after getting this windfall? What would you do in the first five years? Besides items mentioned in the first two answers, how would you spend this money to benefit yourself? How would you spend it to benefit others?

224

Tool #15. On a large sheet of plain paper, using marking pens, pastels, and crayons, draw a field on which you would like to live your work life. Include the people, places, and things you would like in your work life. When your picture is complete, make lists of the skills you would be using at various places on the field. Then, in a dark color, draw fences across your field to indicate the barriers you have created to keep you from getting what you want. Label these barriers. Write a paragraph at the bottom of your field about how you intend to deal with these barriers.

Where Am I Going?

Tool #16. Imagine that you have not seen your closest friend or most dearly loved one in five years, and that you are writing to them now to describe the perfect job, which you have found in the meantime. Use the person's name in the salutation of the letter and then go on to tell them in as much detail as possible all about your work: what you are doing, what your title is (if any), where you are doing this work, with whom, what your days are like, and what parts of this work are particularly joyful to you. Use the last paragraph of the letter to tell this special person your feelings about your work.

Tool #17. Imagine that, like a famous political leader or explorer, you keep a journal. Imagine further that you are writing on a typical day ten years in the future. Describe your day in as much detail as possible. Start with where you wake up, how you start your day, how you get to work (unless you work at the same place you live), what you do at work, who you see, what you notice about your surroundings. Include whatever happens to you during lunch and then comment on your afternoon. Describe how you spend your evening. At the end of your journal entry, write with as much candor as you can muster about your feelings about what you did during the day.

Tool #18. I do not want, in the words of Thoreau, "to discover that I had not lived" as I face death. Nor do you. What do you need to do now in your life so that you will not feel unfulfilled when you reach the end? Write several paragraphs responding to this question.

Tool #19. Imagine that you are your own best friend and that "you" have died and that as the best friend of the deceased, you have been asked to prepare a eulogy. Start by describing the details in the life now completed, then talk about the accomplishments, and finally write about your feelings for your departed friend.

Tool #20. On a separate sheet of paper, write nine things you are going to do as result of reading this book and doing these exercises. Then identify the three most important and label these "A." Pick the three least important and label these "C." Label the three remaining items "B." Find a piece of tape or magnetic holder and attach this priorities list to the door of your refrigerator. This is the doorway to the rest of your life.

APPENDIX B:
TWENTY-QUESTION
CAREER QUIZ

To get a reading on your work life, check one of the five boxes beside each question (almost always, often, sometimes, rarely, almost never). Describe here the work for which you will answer these questions:

_____

_____

_____

_____

_____

_____

_____

_____

_____

1. I talk to friends about jobs and careers. ☐ ☐ ☐ ☐ ☐

2. I am bored by my work. ☐ ☐ ☐ ☐ ☐

3. Friends seem inspired by my attitude toward work. ☐ ☐ ☐ ☐ ☐

4. I feel that I have a clear understanding of my strengths and weaknesses at work. ☐ ☐ ☐ ☐ ☐

5. I am angry at bosses, co-workers, or clients. ☐ ☐ ☐ ☐ ☐

6. I feel excited by my work. ☐ ☐ ☐ ☐ ☐

7. Friends give me information about other work opportunities. ☐ ☐ ☐ ☐ ☐

8. People tell me I do my work well. ☐ ☐ ☐ ☐ ☐

9. I do more work than is required without feeling pushed. ☐ ☐ ☐ ☐ ☐

10. I dislike going to work. ☐ ☐ ☐ ☐ ☐

11. I read about other jobs or careers. ☐ ☐ ☐ ☐ ☐

12. I talk candidly with friends about pleasant and unpleasant parts of my work. ☐ ☐ ☐ ☐ ☐

13. I am on a high about my work. ☐ ☐ ☐ ☐ ☐

14. My work seems to have little meaning. ☐ ☐ ☐ ☐ ☐

15. I am aware of my likes and dislikes at work. ☐ ☐ ☐ ☐ ☐

16. I feel that my work is in perspective with other parts of my life. ☐ ☐ ☐ ☐ ☐

17. I have physical problems from stress at work. ☐ ☐ ☐ ☐ ☐

18. My hobbies and outside interests give me ideas about other kinds of work I might enjoy. ☐ ☐ ☐ ☐ ☐

19. I feel that my work is about right for me. ☐ ☐ ☐ ☐ ☐

20. My work seems more like play than like a job. ☐ ☐ ☐ ☐ ☐

To score, mark points in the spaces below according to the following table, and then add the total in each column.

$$Almost \ never = 1$$
$$Rarely = 2$$
$$Sometimes = 3$$
$$Often = 4$$
$$Almost \ always = 5$$

D Scale	E Scale	R Scale	C Scale
2. __	1. __	3. __	4. __
5. __	7. __	6. __	8. __
10. __	11. __	9. __	12. __
14. __	15. __	13. __	16. __
17. __	18. __	20. __	19. __
__	__	__	__

Interpretation Instructions

The most important factor to consider in interpreting the results of your twenty-question career quiz is that the answers come from you and no one else. They are your response to twenty questions which many others have also considered.

The next thing to notice is that each of us has some involvement at each of the four points measured. Unlike a model train, which is only at one place at a time on a circular track, we have some energy on the D scale (Discontent), E scale (Exploration), R scale (Renewal), and C scale (Consolidation).

The most simple interpretation is that the scale on which you have the most points is where you are, although *your* perception of this is more important than any numbers. You might also look at your results this way:

- If your D scale is higher than your E scale, it may be time to do some more exploring.
- If your D and C scales together are higher than your E and R scales, it may also be an indication that it is time to do more exploring.
- If your E scale is highest, it may be time to shift to exploring which is likely to lead to commitment (probably research meetings).
- If your R and C scales are the highest, you probably consider yourself happy in your work.

Remember, your opinions are more important than the numbers on any scale. If you still want a better understanding of this quiz, go back and look at the statements which apply to each scale (you can determine this by the question numbers in the scoring section). See how these statements apply to you. What other factors are relevant for *you*?

APPENDIX C:
CAREER COUNSELING

There are no whole truths:
All truths are half truths.

ALFRED NORTH WHITEHEAD

The words that follow are for those who seek career counseling and for those who do career counseling, whether informally or professionally. The simple model presented offers guidelines, not an exhaustive analysis, and only aspires to present a piece of the truth, recognizing the wisdom in the words of the Harvard philosopher quoted above.

For those seeking career counseling, this appendix offers an idea of what to expect, including some perspective on how career counseling compares to other kinds of support. This also gives the prospective client some picture of what might happen in career counseling sessions, and some standard by which to evaluate sessions when they are completed.

Those seeking career guidance will recognize that much of what this book encourages you to do for yourself also happens in counseling sessions, a similarity reflecting the same underlying processes. The difference between career counseling and other forms of support, and this can be a significant difference, is that career counseling is *personal* and *individualized:* what happens in a session reflects the needs of the particular client then and there.

The guidelines that follow are based on several assumptions. The most important is the idea made popular by Carl Rogers: the client knows best. In what Rogers calls client-centered therapy (notice that the word "patient" is eliminated), the underlying assumption is that the client is responsible, capable of self-motivated change, and more aware than anyone else of what is best for his or her life. I share this assumption. Related to this basic belief is the idea that the role of the career counselor is to facilitate goal achievement for the client, *not* to judge the client, *not* to impose the counselor's own values on the client, *not* to create a clone of the counselor, *not* to change the client's behavior to become congruent with the counselor's own attitudes and beliefs.

Why?

These assumptions, in my counseling experience, are what works! When clients see their own answers, create their own options, discover their own truths, they act on this knowledge in ways that are truly powerful. They get what they want and they get it, in the final analysis, on their own.

The structure of career counseling, as I see it, involves two basic occurrences in each session and two basic types of relationships between client and counselor.

Each session should have at least two outcomes for the client: a better understanding of where he or she is, and a better understanding of where he or she might go from here. The first involves establishing *context* (from the Latin *contexere*, meaning "to weave or join together"). Many people seek career counseling because they feel lost or alone; somewhere underlying their appeal for help is the assumption that "I am the only one who has this discontent or faces these challenges." The skillful counselor leads the client to see the situation in terms of others who have been in the same position, perhaps using a metaphor like the careercycles map. The client draws hope from the fact that others have become successful, and this reduces fear and anxiety and establishes a foundation of increased confidence for moving forward.

The second outcome involves creating *options* (from the Latin *optio*, meaning "choice"). The skillful counselor integrates the various messages from the client and then leads the client to see that there are choices for action, choices that were not apparent to the client before the session. Just as the client is the source for developing options, the client sets the priorities for acting on the options because, after all, the client will be doing the work. In both cases the counselor guides, suggests, reflects back, but the energy and the inspiration come from the client.

If there is a series of sessions (a big "if," since many clients get what they need in one or two sessions), then the nature of the client/counselor relationship will probably shift from the counselor filling the role of clarifier to counselor in the role of coach. As clarifier, the counselor helps to establish context and create options, as described above, often organizing diverse facts and thoughts and feelings to lead the client to the brink of action. As coach, the counselor still helps to establish context and create options, but the focus is narrower now and the actions more specific. Coaching sessions are often shorter than an hour and may be done over the phone. Where clarifying demands special counseling *skills*, the emphasis in coaching is special *knowledge*. The outcome of coaching sessions, the destination point, is the satisfactory conclusion of a new work agreement for the client.

These elements of the career counseling process come together in a four-phase diagram (Figure 18), shown here with the central question for each of the four phases.

Clarifying, in the sense used here, dates back at least to the 1880 "Case of Anna O," from which Sigmund Freud developed his ideas about talk therapy. We derive value from talking about our life to another, fully attentive, person. We understand ourselves better as the words come forth. Clarity ensues. The healing that Freud sought is combined, in career counseling, with a sharper sense of where we are and where we want to go from here.

Coaching likewise has been studied and analyzed extensively. The magic of coaches like Bear Bryant or John Wooden cannot be fully captured, but we know for certain that large dollops of both knowledge and inspiration are involved. The successful coach, and the successful career counselor, knows the methods for achieving the goal *and* knows how to motivate others to use those methods. Communicated in diverse ways, this combination of knowledge and the will to act on that knowledge leads the athlete, or the career counseling client, on to success.

As this book has made clear, there are a number of sources for help in the world of work; career counseling is

FIGURE 18

Time (minutes) / Time (days) →		Clarifying	Coaching
	Establishing Context	Where am I in my worklife?	Where am I on specific work opportunities?
	Creating Options	What worklife choices do I have?	What choices do I have on specific work opportunities?

Career Counseling Model

only one of them. Whether you seek a better work life using career counseling or one of the other options, the imperative is to act now. The results you produce will make all the difference for you and those around you, and the skills you develop will serve you for the rest of your life.

BIBLIOGRAPHY

Applegath, John. *Working Free: Practical Alternatives to the 9 to 5 Job.* Amacom Press, New York, 1982. Well written, inspiring, informative handbook.

Boll, Carl. *Executive Jobs Unlimited.* Macmillan Publishing, New York, 1965. Fine ideas on resumes (don't) and informational interviews (do).

Bolles, Richard. *What Color is Your Parachute?* Ten Speed Press, Berkeley, annually. Definitive work on job seeking. Thorough, complete, with loads of valuable information.

Bolles, Richard. *Quick Job Hunting Map.* Ten Speed Press, Berkeley, 1979. The best self-administered skills assessment tool (available separately or in **Parachute**).

Bolles, Richard. *The Three Boxes of Life.* Ten Speed Press, Berkeley, 1978. Another thorough and inspiring work, this time on the broader subject of life/work planning.

Burke, Anna Mae. *What do you want to be when you grow up?* Prentice-Hall, Englewood Cliffs, 1982. Readable, practical guide to career choice and job finding.

Campbell, David. *If you don't know where you're going, you'll probably end up somewhere else.* Argus Comm., Niles, Illinois, n.d. Simple and superb. Practical advice on goal setting.

Cowle, Jerry. *How to Survive Getting Fired and Win.* Warner Books, New York, 1979. One man's experience of losing his job and bouncing back.

Donaho, Melvin and Meyer, John. *How to Get the Job You Want.* Prentice-Hall, Englewood Cliffs, 1976. Practical guide to job finding by two professionals.

Figler, Howard. *The Complete Job-Search Handbook.* Holt, Rinehart & Winston, New York, 1979. The whole process, using a twenty skills format.

Gardner, John. *Self-Renewal.* Harper and Row, New York, 1964. Articulate and uplifting view of "the individual and the innovative society."

Garrison, Clifford and others. *Finding a Job You Feel Good About.* Argus Communications, Niles, Illinois, 1977. Simple and effective, with helpful tests and exercises.

German, Richard and Arnold, Peter. *Job and Career Building.* Ten Speed Press, Berkeley, 1980. Specifics on approaching employers and getting job offers.

Hagberg, Janet and Leider, Richard. *The Inventurers: Excursions in Life and Career Renewal.* Addison-Wesley, Reading, Massachusetts, 1978. Humanistic and innovative treatment of lifework planning.

Harkness, Charles. *Career Counseling.* Charles C. Thomas, Springfield, Illinois, 1976. Definitive work for "practitioners and would-be practitioners."

Harragan, Betty. *Games Mother Never Taught You.* Warner Books, New York, 1977. No holds barred view of "corporate gamesmanship for women."

Jackson, Tom. *Guerrilla Tactics in the Job Market.* Bantam Books, New York, 1979. Highly readable and practical approach, with seventy-eight exercises—which work!

Jackson, Tom and Mayleas, Davidyne. *The Hidden Job Market in the '80s.* New York Times Books, New York, 1982. Sound advice, with exercises and questions arranged in a logical job-hunting sequence.

Jongeward, Dorothy and Seyer, Philip. *Choosing Success: TA on the Job.* John Wiley, New York, 1978. Principles of *Born to Win* applied to work.

Lathrop, Richard. *Don't Use a Resume.* Ten Speed Press, Berkeley, 1980. Short, punchy book arguing for the "qualifications brief."

Levinson, Daniel. *The Seasons of a Man's Life.* Alfred A. Knopf, New York, 1976. Valuable insights on adult life stages from in-depth study of forty men.

Levinson, Jay. *Earning Money without a Job.* Holt, Rinehart and Winston, New York, 1979. Clear and helpful view of earning a living working for yourself. Excellent!

Levinson, Jay. *555 Ways to Earn Extra Money.* Holt, Rinehart and Winston, New York, 1982. More good ideas on "economic freedom."

Maccoby, Machael. *The Gamesman.* Simon & Schuster, New York, 1976. New vocabulary for how we achieve organizational success.

McGregor, Douglas. *The Human Side of Enterprise.* Theory X and Theory Y *still* provide excellent perspective on management style.

Moore, Charles Guy. *The Career Game.* Ballantine Books, New York, 1976. Innovative and thorough treatment of the career development process.

O'Neil, George and Nena. *Shifting Gears.* Avon Books, New York, 1974. Psychological insight and practical advice from two who see career development as a life process.

Phillips, Michael. *The Seven Laws of Money.* Random House, New York, 1974. Wonderful and original ideas on a hot topic; easy to read and worth it.

Potter, Beverly. *Beating Job Burnout.* Grosset & Dunlap, New York, 1982. Thoughtful treatment full of practical advice, evaluative tools, and exercises.

Rogers, Edward. *Getting Hired.* Prentice-Hall, Englewood Cliffs, 1982. Articulate advice for college students interested in the advertising business.

Rohrlich, Jay. *Work and Love: The Crucial Balance.* Summit Books, New York, 1980. Scholarly yet readable review of work and its abuses.

Sheehy, Gail. *Passages.* Bantam Books, New York, 1977. Synthesis of much of the thinking on adult life stages.

Terkel, Studs. *Working.* Avon Books, New York, 1974. Diverse interviews interspersed with wise words from a guru of work.

Thompson, Barbara. *Working Whenever You Want.* Prentice-Hall, Englewood Cliffs, 1983. Definitive work on temporary employment: thorough, clear, logical, excellent!

Vaillant, George. *Adaptation to Life.* Little, Brown & Co., Boston, 1977. Articulate and applicable life stages study based on Harvard graduates of the '40s.

Weber, Max. *The Protestant Ethic and the Spirit of Capitalism.* (translated by Talcott Parsons) Charles Scribner's Sons,

New York, 1958. Seminal thinking on attitudes toward work in industrialized nations.

Weinrach, Stephen (editor). *Career Counseling: Theoretical and Practical Perspectives.* McGraw-Hill, New York, 1979. Thoughtfully structured and thorough collection of articles.

INDEX